THE MINDFUL PHOTOGRAPHY FIELD GUIDE

THE MINDFUL PHOTOGRAPHY FIELD GUIDE

15 Smartphone Photography Practices for Inner Peace

Joe Van Wyk

The Mindful Photography Field Guide:
15 Smartphone Photography Practices for Inner Peace

ISBN: 979-8-9903971-0-1

Joe Van Wyk LLC
JoeVanWyk.com   MindfulPhotography.org
Printed in the United States of America

*To the friends who supported me
while I found gratitude for life, as-is.
You are God with skin on.*

CONTENTS

ACKNOWLEDGEMENTS

Allow me a moment to express my gratitude for the people and circumstances that led to this idea becoming reality.

GOD

Jesus, sometimes I think back to me in childhood, dressed up singing out of the hymnal. One particular song, "In the Garden," would become the best description of my relationship with you over the years. In the refrain we sang:

"And He walks with me, and He talks with me, and He tells me I am His own."

While I sometimes sense you walking and talking with me during my daily, multi-tasking rush, you have shown me another far more predictable place to be with you: in the place of presence. When I hum the unmistakable melody of "In the Garden," I land on the opening words and smile:

I come to the garden alone, While the dew is still on the roses; And the voice I hear, falling on my ear, The Son of God discloses.

So I thank you my friend and savior, that your spirit is forever within this moment, never failing. In desperate times I cried out to you, yelled at you, and even shook my fist at you in blame. Yet here you have remained, every fresh morning in the garden, telling me that I am Yours.

FAMILY

Mom, this book was published just a few months after you went to be with the Lord. It makes my heart smile that you are with Dad in Heaven together. Dad, please forgive me for poking fun at your color challenges in the "No Matchy" chapter. Your Heavenly outfits surely clash in brilliant and lovable ways.

Even recently I have talked with the two of you down in my spirit, asking for guidance. Each time I close my eyes and put my attention on the two of you, I see your faces smiling and nodding at me, urging me to press onward with Mindful Photography. One time in tearful prayer, it felt like each of you had a hand on my shoulders. Imagine that. Even now, you two never give up on me.

Bill, Laura, and John, you each play such an important role in my life. I'm so grateful that God placed me in this world as your little brother. We are each so different, yet equally impacted by growing up in Mom's and Dad's loving home.

Sara, my sister-in-law and life coach, you have had a powerful influence on me. The creative and emotional growth I have experienced with you saved my life. The bond of trust combined with action-minded accountability I have with you is beyond any traditional therapy I wasted money on.

And Caleb, my precious son, your Dad couldn't love you more or be any prouder of you. I know you inherited a bit of my cray-cray, so I have to apologize for that; just be glad you got your Mom's good looks. Sometimes I think our odd way of viewing this crazy life is what enables us to have our marathon phone calls and hilarious interactions. God not only gave me a son, but he gave me a trusted friend too. I love you buddy.

MENTORS, TEACHERS, AND FAITH PARTNERS

God has always put powerful men of faith in my life who have served roles like friends, mentors, sponsors, pastors, and study partners. We men genuinely need to build each other up in faith, courage, loving-camaraderie, and of course, inappropriate jokes. The groups I have been involved with among radically honest men convinced me that I'm not alone in my struggles with false identifications and dependencies. As iron sharpens iron, we friends sharpen each other.

Thank you to the phenomenal artists and teachers who have lit me up over the years. Bruce Gilden, when I saw your outrageous, in-their-face street shots I was blown away. Thank God I didn't get killed trying to mimic your photographic style. Eric Kim, you are the most prolific street photography writer ever. Thank you for your workshops and influence on my photography. Same to you, Thorsten Overgaard. You guys are so hard working and dedicated to this craft. To all of my life's creative teachers, thank you pushing the envelope and showing what's possible.

Dawn Josephson, my trusted book-writing coach and editor, thank you for the heart-connection I have with you. Thank you for your deep wisdom and experience. Thank you for celebrating this project; your energy has helped me persevere.

SUFFERING

Jesus said it plainly: "In this world you will have trouble." Through these practices, you will join me in cooperating with life's troubles a little more, and fighting them a little less. We are promised peace in the world we live in. It is difficult to experience that mysterious peace while we are battling with our problems.

Friends, we are in this together. Suffering is part of the human experience, but it doesn't have to be the whole of our experience. Wallowing in self-pity is enticing, but kicking our fears in the ass is far more fun. Let's capture some adventures together. I promise you'll find moments of divine inner peace along the way.

Blessings,
Joe

THE MINDFUL PHOTOGRAPHY FIELD GUIDE

JOE VAN WYK AND FRANKIE THE DOODLE
ROARING FORK VALLEY, COLORADO

INTRODUCTION

Years ago, during a dark period in my life, I realized that while I was practicing photography I wasn't dwelling on my problems. I was getting a taste of present-moment awareness and what that feels like in my body. As a result, I gained courage to sit with tough emotions without judging them or myself. That felt empowering. Challenges with depression and anxiety forced me to discard outdated and ineffective beliefs and to instead implement tools that actually work for me, bringing me inner peace in the present.

STATEMENT OF AUTHENTICITY

The words in this book are from me and my lived experience. AI was not used to create this copy. The photos are taken with various iPhones over the span of years. The few exceptions are noted in the copy. AI was not used to generate these images. The illustrations used are created from licensed artwork. I designed and produced the book.

WARNING: METAPHOR ALERT

There is something curious about throwing a frame around an object or scene. It focuses our attention on that which is within the frame.

Part of the therapeutic value of mindful photography is that it utilizes our smartphone's photographing, editing, and sending capabilities. As I acknowledge, sticking the words "mindful" and "smartphone" together is quite the oxymoron. We will mitigate some of the distractions of constant connectedness by using our smartphone cameras with airplane mode on and Wi-Fi off.

But even then, sometimes I just like to leave the distraction device at home while I go for a walk with Frankie the Doodle. Instead of the phone, I'll throw an old-fashioned 35 mm slide frame into my pocket for the ultimate in minimalistic camera experiences. Yep, I'm the weird guy caught by passers-by using a tiny imaginary camera.

The closer the white slide frame gets to my eyeball, the wider the view. The further away the frame, the tighter the view—almost like the frame is a macro lens. But, it's all fictitious, right? It's just a mental fantasy after all. I'm not *actually* taking a photograph, so what's the point?

My answer to that question is in the form of a challenge: try it for yourself. Even now, with your left hand, close one eye, make the OK gesture with your fingers, and frame that circle around an object in front of you. Try some cool angles. Do it for just a second or two.

Congratulations. I hope you "photographed" a pleasing image because it's probably stuck in your brain for now. See how that works?

In our little exercise we focus on an object but we could just as well have been focusing on and observing our thoughts. If you were to throw a frame around the cluster of thoughts you are experiencing now, what would you observe? Do your current thoughts look like a cross between a fun-house and a horror show? No need to call for help. Your thoughts are not your reality. You are going to learn to just sit with them and in the process, you'll show them who's boss. During these practices, we will keep coming back to the shot at hand, to the present, visual moment. Most likely, we'll discover that the now is a pretty decent place to be. And, it was right here all along—a place to find peace amidst the circus show in our heads.

NOTE TO FELLOW HIGHLY SENSITIVE SOULS

I want you to know that I understand what you are experiencing. If you've been labeled "treatment resistant," or branded in any way, trust me, there is a way out of the loop of hopelessness.

A decade ago, a fateful event would happen in my life, and I would be reconnected to a former love. What seemed like a miraculous answer to my needy prayers turned into the darkest period of my life. Before that marriage ended, I had been through the deepest hell of depression that I had ever experienced. "Team Joe," full of the usual players in the mental health industry, like psychiatrists, therapists, clinics, and of course pharmacies, tried everything to fix my mysterious problem. We tried in vain to medicate, shock, transfuse, and group-therapy my discontent, but I always wound up back where I started: depressed and desperately wanting to check out permanently.

God bless them—I had single-handedly stumped the experts of modern psychiatric medicine. Of course for me, that sucked big-time, because I was now out of options.

MY TRUTH

It took going into the depths of emotional hell for me to discover that I was not a diagnosis or a problem to be fixed. I was born a highly sensitive child. That is how I was created for my unique mission. My journey to freedom would become the will to live out the unique role and path that God designed for me. The goal would now be to stop fighting God's will and way. To turn from obsessing on the self, and instead, to actively bless others while I use my gifts.

THE QUAGMIRE

There is a built-in predicament in every therapeutic attempt to relieve sadness and suffering. While we are down, we tend to resist doing the things that make us feel better. The mind has a peculiar way of always retreating back to the equilibrium of the doldrums. The familiar funk is an ever present magnet. Personally, I discovered photography to be a therapeutic tool that worked long-term for me because of the pleasurable feelings I experience while I am creating photographs and sharing images with those I can bless. These practices are created for people who get the tingles over photography. That love of the art compels us to act opposite to our emotions and to go out and get lost in presence, manifesting beautiful things.

A DIFFERENT FLAVOR OF MINDFULNESS TEACHINGS

As you might have guessed by now, these mindfulness practices are going to have a different vibe than hot-body yoga class and crystal aromatherapy. Practicing mindful photography will be an active, engaging, and challenging experience out in the wild. The practices are born out of powerful therapeutic methods that emphasize active, tactile, engaging interventions for people who suffer from challenging emotions.

We can all grow in our unique beliefs and practices. I'm open about how my Christian faith has been transformed through developing these teachings of presence. Go into these practices boldly, expecting to deepen your relationship with your Higher Power.

MAKE IT YOUR OWN

You are going to see lots of images of my, *ahem*, handsome face—as well as that of Frankie the Doodle. You'll get a glimpse into my personal journey. But, these teachings must become about *you* and *your* recovery. Substitute yourself for the shots of me, and your own furry friend for the shots of Frankie. Give each practice a try, then create your own unique variations. I'd be honored if this book lived either inside your backpack, or on the back of the toilet.

Through practicing mindful photography, your motivation to capture and share images will change. Your visual sense will become a powerful tool in the moment that brings you back to your source of inner peace.

Blessings,
Joe

PART I

WHY MINDFUL PHOTOGRAPHY?

A WORLD IN CRISIS

Why, despite our technological and medical achievements, are depression and anxiety at record levels in our society? Why do so many struggle with loneliness and isolation, despite having abundant on-screen friends and countless ways to stay in touch?

Traditional models of treatment and pharmaceuticals have failed us because they tend to focus on diagnosis and symptom management rather than giving people new life tools that can help alleviate the root of the issues. Religion has failed us too (or better yet, we have failed religion). We all have a natural tendency to allow our belief systems to construct walls around us that further our feelings of isolation and block us from true intimacy with God and our fellows. Additionally, AI-refined algorithms amplify our discontent, leaving us unsatisfied but scrolling for more. Wouldn't it be better to enjoy the abundant blessings currently all around us?

Do you feel like you are at the mercy of your self-defeating thoughts? Are you at a crisis point in your own life right now, hurting from unfulfilled dreams and feelings that society is falling apart? Do you feel like you have "tried everything" and that you're running out of options to find contentment?

THE WHY:

There are 700,000 deaths per year by suicide.[1]
WORLD HEALTH ORGANIZATION

For every suicide completion, there are 25 attempts.[2]
MERCK MANUALS

In the U.S., white males are 30% of the population
but make up 70% of deaths by suicide.[3]
AMERICAN FOUNDATION FOR SUICIDE PREVENTION

Suicide is the 2nd leading cause of death
for people ages 10-34.[4]
CENTERS FOR DISEASE CONTROL AND PREVENTION

Suicide is the 2nd leading cause of death
among veterans under 45.[5]
U.S. DEPARTMENT OF VETERAN AFFAIRS

You are not alone. I have felt that way too. A crisis of faith forced me to get serious about the whole "be here now" thing. I knew I had to learn to be okay with my God, myself, and my current situation or I would never find the "peace which transcends all understanding" that my faith promises.

A CRISIS OF FAITH

This brings us back to the original question posed in the title: Why mindful photography? In short, I was in bad shape and desperate to have a life worth living. I suffered years of vain attempts to find God in beliefs and things, versus love and presence. I became mighty depressed as a result.

Back then, I systematically approached my challenging emotions as if I were a problem in need of a fix. But now, I radically accept that, while my intense feelings are sometimes hard to live with, God created me this way to fulfill my destiny. As it turns out, my high sensitivity benefits me greatly. Being empathic, I have a large capacity for love. I can create beautiful things. Most importantly, I can connect with and bless suffering people because of the journey I have walked.

Before we get too far, allow me to be transparent about my beliefs. First, I'm a follower of Jesus, so that would label me a Christian. But, remember, labels are just a mental construct. I have no desire to preach to you or convert you to my way of thinking. These teachings emphasize the importance of you finding the path that fits you and produces inner peace amidst life's storms.

Like people of all religions, Christians come in many varieties. Just look at the many denominations and Bible translations, and how many lame jokes Christians tell about each other, and you'll see how diverse this one group of people can be. I still chuckle when I think back to my childhood in my hometown Baptist church. About an hour into the service the preacher would say, "No need to look at your watches, folks. The Methodists have already beat us to lunch."

Many Christians like me grew up in a culture that valued fellowshipping, evangelizing, solving problems, competing, building things, and working our butts off. In that culture it was natural to become a human *doing* versus a human *being*.

When I was in my late-20s, I reached a point when the go-go faith of my childhood no longer met my need for peace. My overactive mind produced frightening, intrusive thoughts, and I wanted them to go away. No amount of praying and rebuking could silence the non-stop chatter. I began to seek out every resource I knew of to fix me so that I might change my circumstances and be happy at last.

Growing more desperate, I ran out of options to solve my problems. Finally, I reached my spiritual bottom. That's what it took for me to realize I wasn't a problem to fix, a disorder to medicate, or a diagnosis in need of a cure.

I met Christians in the contemplative tradition who were disciplined in their meditation practices. I started practicing Centering Prayer, a silent form of prayer created in the 70s by Father Thomas Keating and fellow Trappist monks in response to the influx of Asian meditation methods. I finally got a taste of stillness—of slip-

ping into that mysterious place of calm awareness. I was experiencing peace with unsolved problems.

Eastern teachings also found me through Dialectical Behavioral Therapy (DBT), a transformational course that I took years back. DBT's highly practical, hands-on therapeutic approaches are great inspirations for many of these mindful photography practices. I always loved one DBT tip: Are you so far out on an emotional limb that the idea of a mindful intervention is out of reach? Repeatedly stick your face in a bowl of ice. Folks, that's what you call an attitude adjustment.

Central to practical DBT teachings is the idea of "dialectics," and the concept that we can hold two seemingly opposite things in each hand, with both being perfectly true and valid. I was first exposed to the Zen idea of Shoshin, or beginner's mind. It sounded a lot like the familiar teaching of Jesus when he taught that the only way to enter the Kingdom of Heaven (pure consciousness) is to become like children (humble and teachable).

My experience with God started to change.

Grand Staircase–Escalante National Monument, Utah

THE GOD WITH BILLIONS OF DEFINITIONS

Each of our own spiritual beliefs is as unique as our individual fingerprints. We are complex, multi-faceted beings, with our own stories and perceptions. I'm a Christian, but I have never met another Christian with my same exact take on God, scripture, or life. Plus, people outside of my childhood faith, who had a peace that I admired and wanted in myself, have profoundly influenced my life and my thinking. So this begs the question: "What undeniable fact is sensed by all humans?" Consciousness seems to be the most universal answer to that. We generally agree that awareness is the essential part of being human. Mindfulness is about practicing that awareness, or presence. The miracle of it is that while mindfulness benefits our own emotional health and that of people around us, it also enriches our diverse experiences with God.

MINDFULNESS IS FOUND IN ALL THE MAJOR WORLD RELIGIONS

While few of us agree on personal descriptions of a Higher Power, the majority of us do indeed believe in a higher power—9 in 10 in the U.S.[6] How about you?

In the U.S., mindfulness tends to be taught from a secular perspective. But, so many faith traditions point towards deep presence as a portal to a divine and peaceful energy. In the Old Testament Psalms are the assuring words, "Be still, and know that I am God." An important aspect of Islam is Dhikr, meaning remembrance of our innate knowledge of God. Kavanah in Judaism are teachings about a worshiper's mental and emotional absorption during prayers. Samadhi in Buddhism and Hinduism is a state of total absorptive contemplation in the absolute.

Who or what is your Higher Power? Can you answer that clearly? Until you can clearly define your personal sense of God, Universal Truth, Source, or Collective Conscience, it is challenging to tease out which of the stories bouncing around in your head are inspired by divine sunshine, and which are inspired by the enchiladas you had at lunch.

Once you make your choice and align with your own True North, you will naturally let go of limiting stories. Miraculous ones will take their place. This happened a century ago in a moment of destiny.

BILL AND EBBY

Back in the 1930s, one of the most life-impacting encounters of the 20th century occurred in a humble kitchen in Brooklyn, New York. Bill Wilson, who would become co-founder of Alcoholics Anonymous, jittered at the kitchen table across from a fresh-faced former drunk named Ebby. The last thing Bill wanted was this new religious convert to start preaching to him about God. But then, his friend Ebby simply suggested what seemed like a novel idea to Bill: "Why don't you choose your own conception of God?"

That lightning bolt moment for Bill Wilson transported him from religious victim to the author of his own definition of God. From that came the "God, as we understand God" idea in the Twelve Steps that has welcomed people who felt previously burned, baffled, or unwelcome in mainstream religion.

We humans make things so complicated. Sometimes it's nice to hold on to memorable basic principles that will be available to us through thick and thin, as these principles shape our outlook on life. Our beliefs are our choice. Let's try one of those beliefs on for size and see how it grabs you.

"GOD IS FOR YOU."

Do you resist that statement? Sometimes I struggle with it because I look back at difficult times in my life and my lower self wants to blame God for unpleasant circumstances of the past. That always takes me to my shadow self, and that's definitely not my pathway to inner peace.

When I'm feeling down, I strive to acknowledge that even Jesus spoke the undeniable truth that there will be trouble in this world. And, he also declared that "in Him" we may have peace. That may mean different things to different people. "In Him" might be interpreted as consciousness or a deep state of presence. Others might know "in Him" during an act of praise or speaking in tongues. Some say it means "through the Savior." Regardless, when you choose to interact with a Higher Power whom you decide is *for* you, not *against* you, your whole outlook on life changes.

MINDFULNESS: DEFINING THE UNDEFINABLE

Mindfulness goes by many names: consciousness, awareness, the present, the now, and stillness. "Waking up" into a mindful state of awareness takes practice.

In the ninth century, the Buddhist sage Lin Chi told a monk, "If you meet the Buddha on the road, kill him." He meant that those who think they've found all the answers in any religion or physical idol need to start questioning.

Mindfulness cannot be described; it must be experienced. Any attempts to define it are downright silly. How can we explain consciousness? Consciousness is the eternal mystery of life.

WHAT DOES IT FEEL LIKE TO BE ALIVE IN A MINDFUL STATE, VERSUS LOST IN THE THINKING STATE?

The thinking state is a powerful gravitational force. Call us cursed or just plain bonkers, but our lower self gravitates towards the misery of the thinking state. Eckhart Tolle calls it the "pain body." The Apostle Paul referred to the "flesh." Carl Jung wrote of the "shadow." However we define it, our propensity to "go negative" is so

MINDFUL STATE	THINKING STATE
Conscious	*Unconscious*
Awake	*Asleep*
Lost in Creation	*Lost in Thought*
Feelings in the Body	*Obsessions in the Mind*
Aware of Senses	*Detached from Reality*
Living in the Present	*Regretting in Past*
Humble (Beginner's Mind)	*Prideful*

automatic that it takes a radical commitment to bring about lasting change. The good news is, using photography as a means for mindfulness is effective because it is creative, gets you into a "feeling" state, and most of all, is really fun.

The process of mindful photography opens our senses up to the reality surrounding us. Many people seek to transcend the waking dream-state of thought they live in 99% of the time. New mindful photography practitioners invariably get that cheek-to-cheek grin when they drop down into their own bodies for a few seconds, freed of their minds, and observe the miracle of life around them through their senses.

WHY SMARTPHONE PHOTOGRAPHY?

I realize that mindful smartphone photography sounds like an oxymoron.

On one hand, we have the mind-blowing advancement of smartphone cameras. On the other hand, we are balancing the fact that smartphones are society's number one killer of presence (and advertisers' top choice for controlling our minds). However, with discipline, we can take a mindful approach

Instant film cameras are perhaps the most mindful of all. I love how simple the controls are, and the surprise that arrives after each carefully-crafted shot.

to our smartphones too. As such, each practice in this book starts with the intentional act of turning your smartphone into a camera, turning on airplane mode, and cutting off your outside connection while you are practicing.

The exercises in this book will help you master the amazing camera that's always with you. You'll practice photographic awareness, scenes, macro-photography, landscapes, abstracts, architecture, street photography, portraiture, approaching strangers, editing, organizing, and archiving your work.

Do you prefer using your big-kid camera? Wonderful. Believe me, I'm not putting my fancy gear on eBay anytime soon. I encourage you to mix things up. Sometimes I go out with my instant camera. It's so fun watching mindfully-composed shots as they slowly appear in that classic white frame. On special occasions I'll take a day trip and shoot a roll of film with my old rangefinder. Heck, I frequently go on walks with no camera at all, instead opting for the simple old slide holder, framing and taking mental snapshots here and there.

In the following pages, you will learn the art of seeing like you've never seen before. You will discover new angles and details you never noticed. And, I assure you that while you are mindfully and methodically creating images, your obsessive mind will catch a much-needed break.

WHAT ABOUT VIDEO?

I am bullish on smartphone video. These days, I trust my top-end iPhone for just about any video content creation project.

But here's the thing: for those of you who don't know it, video is a major pain in the butt.

We will learn more about mitigating some of the perils of shooting photos with our smartphones by "turning our smartphones into cameras" before going on a mindful shoot. Properly insulated from distractions, we shoot and edit several mindful still shots, sending them off to someone with an "I love you." Simple simple.

Video on the other hand, can raise the distraction level of mindful shooting to eleven. Instead of one single frame in the case of a still photo, a video is thousands of frames, with much more cerebral intensity.

In order for these practices to be effective, you must make them your own. Experiment, and most of all, have fun. Keep on checking in on your inner body, and do what you are drawn to. Do what makes you get lost in time.

For me personally, going out and babbling a selfie vertical video message doesn't feel like a "mindful video." On the other hand, sitting on the warm beach at water's edge, catching some landscape-oriented slow-mo of shore-breaks coming towards me—well, that feels mindful.

PRACTICE

Mindful Photography is a therapeutic technique designed to relieve suffering through presence. I created these teachings and exercises to help you attain quick and lasting relief from worry and fear, while developing present moment awareness. Your part? Practice. Commit to routinely showing up and cultivating your connection to the Divine.

Remember the old saying "practice makes perfect"? That might be true for bowling and rocket launches, but when it comes to managing your monkey mind, perfection is a perilous goal. The sobering fact is that we are all powerless over the arising of emotions. But, there is hope: your response.

You can access tremendous wisdom and power when you practice sitting with and positively responding to strong feelings. There is nothing to achieve.

MINDFULNESS IS AN ACQUIRED TASTE

It's a slow, home-cooked meal versus a fast food, eat-on-your-lap experience. Fast food gets the job done but it isn't exactly peaceful, and the cleanup is disgusting.

As you embark on these practices, keep your face towards God. Be present now. Everything else is a distraction. Your life is happening at this very moment and nowhere else. What is laid out in front of you this very day is your path. Abandon yesterday's baggage and give up trying to control tomorrow.

Roll up your sleeves, wipe off your lens, and get ready to be transformed by the renewing of your mind.

MINDFULNESS FACTS

OUR MIND HAS THE CAPACITY TO PROCESS 126 PIECES OF INFORMATION EVERY SECOND

Yikes! Talk about TMI or "too much information." Research by Mihaly Csikszentmihalyi, author of the psychological concept of the mental "flow" state, suggests that the supercomputer between our ears is processing vastly more information than we are consciously aware of.[7] Mindfulness helps us give that processor a rest.

TAKE COMFORT: "PRESENT MOMENTS" TYPICALLY LAST FOR JUST 1-10 SECONDS

Research by Daniel Stern has found that our experiences of an uninterrupted now are moments that typically last 1-10 seconds, with some exceptions for very experienced meditators.[8]

MINDFULNESS IMPROVES MOODS

With US marines preparing for deployment, researchers observed that practicing mindfulness meditation in highly stressful and emotional situations allowed meditators to stay alert and in the moment almost as if they were wearing a suit of mental armor. The results show improvements in stress recovery and vital functions, with important implications for evidence-based mental health research and treatment.[9]

CHANGE YOUR BRAIN IN 8 WEEKS

Harvard neuroscientist Sara Lazar discovered that meditation can change your brain's gray matter and neural pathways after just eight weeks. The amygdala, the fight or flight part of the brain that is important for anxiety, fear, and stress in general, actually got smaller.[10]

PART II

THE 3 STEPS OF MINDFUL PHOTOGRAPHY

*"You can't think your way into right action,
but you can act your way into right thinking."*

BILL WILSON

HOPE IN ACTION

I don't know about you, but I can't find God with a searchlight while I'm worrying about the future or regretting the past. The deeper into the worry and regret thought-spiral I go, the more vulnerable I am to self-centered fear. Attempting to control difficult emotions makes matters worse. And then, left to my own devices, I reach the end of the road: hopelessness.

And all of that can happen on a walk to the mailbox and back.

Are you a highly sensitive person? Do words like "artistic," "colorful," "creative," "original," "intuitive," "discerning," and "empathic" describe you? Me too. I know what it's like to experience the world intensely. Sometimes it's a blast, like the way our souls come alive when love is in the air—or how we can completely lose ourselves in a creative project—or when we are brought to tears of joy while walking through a cool fall forest.

All highlights have their shadows, of course, and sensitive people know this all too well. While we know all the joys I just described, we also know what it's like to walk into a room and feel the overwhelm of so many different energies present there. Most people have one single "antenna," but we have a whole body full of them aimed in every direction. Sensory overload can be exhausting, can't it?

QUIRKY, SENSITIVE, WORLD-CHANGER PERSONALITIES, THERE IS HOPE

The Creator designed you this way to fulfill your mission in life. Believe it or not, your battle with depressive and anxious thoughts can become your greatest gift. Desperation has a way of cutting through the BS and reaching truth. The hard-core truth might be phrased as a question: Would you rather have everything you want, or want everything you have? If you are wise enough to choose the latter, then you will intuitively know the value of present moment awareness. Being here right now, recognizing blessings all around you: that's the prize.

Friend, you can sit with a machine-gun fire of rapid thoughts in your mind without turning tail and running (acting out, checking out, freaking out). You can respond to heavy thoughts and unpleasant body sensations with an "aha!" and think of them as the "red light on the dashboard," reminding you to return to presence. A mindful photography intervention is possible at pretty much any waking moment—even without a camera (think: "visual snapshot").

You are not the victim of any diagnosis, disorder, or genetic predisposition. Period. You are a child of God with access to supernatural power—nothing less. At each moment of emotional crisis, you have inside you the quantum strength to feel tough emotions and take positive action regardless of the outside circumstances. Fretting and wallowing can be a form of avoidance behavior. That's why the decision to "act our way into right thinking" is a sacrifice of self-will.

MINDFUL PHOTOGRAPHY BRINGS INNER PEACE THROUGH YOUR MOST POWERFUL SENSE: VISION

Your eyesight can be a portal to peaceful awareness available to you right here, right now.

You can experience the Kingdom of Heaven inside yourself and the Glory of Creation surrounding you. But, there's a catch. All the peace and power of the Universe is available to you only in the here and now. There is no jibber-jabber in the now. No commentaries, judgments, or opinions.

Mindful photography can mean a lot of things. What I'm sharing with you is what has worked for me. This is not yoga-pants and scented-candles mindfulness. Instead, I'm inviting you to roll up your sleeves and put on your leather work gloves. Turning from fear takes courage, but remember, courage leads to victory. These practices are designed to help you realize your divinity, transcending overwhelming emotions. Your mind and body might rage, yet you'll keep breathing into the now, which is where the presence of God exists.

For example, suppose you are walking out of a meeting with the boss, reeling from a comment she made about downsizing. Yikes! Sounds like an opportunity for a spontaneous mindful photography walk around the block. You'll learn to do a little "heart-check" now and then, to notice your body's pleasant reactions to presence.

Or, let's say you are feeling heart-sick and decide to go on a hike. Here you are, doing something positive, yet all you can think about is the last time you were on this trail with your ex-love. Boom! Time to feel those unpleasant body sensations, engage the present moment, and get to shooting (the camera that is).

1 FOCUS
on body and surroundings

2 CAPTURE
the present moment

3 SHINE
your light on someone

Practices can be a planned thing too—like ending a peaceful morning quiet time with a mindful photography gratitude walk through the garden. Or better yet, scheduling one of these 15 practices per week for the next 15 weeks. You might enlist an accountability partner like a friend, mentor, or therapist. Talking through a set of mindful photography photos with someone you trust can be a cathartic experience.

My cluttered mind needs a simple way to remember the mindful photography process. Hence, the formulation of "Focus, Capture, Shine." I start by focusing on my body sensations and surroundings. Then, with my smartphone turned into a camera, I allow presence to envelop me as I capture a photo of this moment. I'm shooting and editing photos just for the immersive visual experience. Finally, I shine my light, making a loving connection with someone simply to bless their moment.

PRACTICE INSTRUCTIONS

*"Practice praiseworthy things and
the God of Peace will be with you."*

PHILIPPIANS 4:9

Notice it says "practice," not "achieve."

Give me more than three instructions at a time and you've lost me. How about you? Remember, peace is the prize, and peace happens in the now. Fretting about whether you're doing these practices "correctly" defeats the purpose. That's just more judgment.

I designed these "Focus, Capture, Shine" instructions specifically to help me when I notice I'm out of whack. Don't worry about memorizing my exact way of doing these practices. When in doubt, just pull on your walking shoes, go out, and practice this therapeutic form of photography. Before long you will discover your own unique practice of mindful photography, available at any time.

1. FOCUS on body and surroundings

• HAND ON HEART • 3 BELLY BREATHS • NOTE YOUR LEVEL OF PEACE • OPEN YOUR EYES

I need to do just something to get closer to your soul
And you do know that I want you
Let's dance, let's shout
Shake your body down to the ground

"SHAKE YOUR BODY (DOWN TO THE GROUND)"
BY THE JACKSONS

When Jackson brothers Randy and Michael wrote this song in the late 70s, I doubt that God was the subject of their lyrics. But if you think about it, it's a perfect formula for engaging with the Almighty.

Truth: You are more mindful while dancing a goofy moon-walk at a wedding reception than while sitting properly on your zafu meditation cushion worrying about yourself. Dancing like no one is watching is "being present in the body." Self-absorbed worry is "being lost in the head."

I'm going to drop some abstract concepts on you about the whole "being in the body" thing. You'll get frequent reminders to "return to the body" and "be where your feet are." Why? Because the more you get out of your head and into your body, the more inner peace you'll experience. In fact, you cannot reach a mindful state of present moment awareness from the mind. How ironic. It really should be called "bodyfulness" instead of "mindfulness."

For those of you who don't know what the heck I'm talking about, please hang with me. When you open your heart, you can receive life-altering messages. The experience of "being in the body" sure was for me.

If "presence" is the desired result, then we need to know what presence actually feels like. Personally, when I was first exposed to the exercises I'm going to detail for you, I was blown away. It was like a portal to a sixth sense had opened. I started pinpointing feelings in my body and was soon able to notice when I had been mentally hijacked even while experiencing emotional dysregulation. I urge you to give these exercises a try.

THE HAND AND ARMCHAIR

This exercise was inspired by Eckhart Tolle. To this day I can remember where I was walking when I heard these "hand and armchair" instructions in one of his audiobooks. I was in mental anguish at the time, willing to try just about anything. Minutes later, I sat down on a chair in a city park and made a new discovery about where the Holy Spirit resides. I didn't have to think about it. I could experience the Holy Spirit by just focusing my awareness on a different place: my body.

Ready? Sit in a way where your wrists are supported and your hands are suspended without touching anything. Next, close your eyes and take a couple of conscious breaths. Ask yourself, "How can I know my right hand is there?" Do you feel the awareness in your hand? Let that expand to your other hand, and to your chest. Breathe into different parts of your body where you feel sensations. You see, the body has an intelligence of its own, outside of the brain. It performs way more functions than a brain alone could handle. All our body's cells store energy and instructions. I suppose we can conclude that God is everywhere, from the deepest recesses of the Universe, to the most microscopic of cells.

THE BODY KEEPS THE SCORE

In his seminal book *The Body Keeps the Score*[11], trauma expert Bessel van der Kolk, MD, shows how trauma affects both the mind and the body. Trauma can shock the body, causing later fight and flight responses to events that pose no true danger. The body remembers past trauma even if we're unaware of it.

Have you ever noticed that we point to our body as the place where our soul resides, not to our head? Take it from someone who has tried in vain to think his way out of mental turmoil. It doesn't work.

Over and over during these practices, as thoughts grab your attention, gently turn your focus back to your body sensations and sense perceptions.

Each Mindful Photography practice will give specific "Focus, Capture, Shine" instructions. We'll begin each emotional intervention by focusing on our body and surroundings.

HERE'S A SCENARIO:

You're at an airport, mid-afternoon, during a holiday weekend. You are daydreaming about someone special waiting back home, greeting you soon with a cold beer and bunny ears (or a bottle of your favorite wine and boxer shorts).

And then the fantasy comes to a screeching halt.

"Ladies and gentlemen, flight 687 has been canceled." Your body core tightens up, your heart pounds, and your mind races. A chain-reaction of "what-ifs" activates. In short, your body starts doing its thing: panic automatically.

This is what I refer to as the "red light on the dashboard." When you're cruising down the highway and that sucker lights up, there is no second-guessing. You pull over as soon as possible.

HAND ON HEART, BELLY BREATHS

Whether you're in our airport scenario, at the office, or on a family outing, when the red light on your dashboard is telling you that you've reached your emotional limit, try this:

Get to a place where you can safely sit or lean, and either close your eyes or blur your gaze. Gently place your hand on your heart, and take a few belly breaths. Simply feel your various body sensations without commentary. Feeling pressure in your scrunched face? Noticing tightness in the front of your chest? Let the thoughts rage. Just notice body sensations. Don't try to change anything. Feel your heartbeat under your right palm.

OPEN YOUR EYES

As you open your eyes, note your level of peace. Keep it simple. Personally, I like to gently pat my heart. If I'm fairly stable, I might pat my heart once or twice. If I'm low on peace, I might pat my heart several times. This important step anchors certain body sensations to your level of inner peace, helping to objectify them and lessen their traumatic charge.

Where are you? What surrounds you? Is your butt touching a chair? Are your feet touching the ground? What sounds do you hear? What is moving and what isn't? Which lights are brightest? What is that smell? Are you feeling warm or chilly?

In film making, your surroundings are called a "scene," or a section of the film in a single location and time. Through your senses, when you note the scene you are in right now, you will intervene in thought.

WELCOME TO THE REAL WORLD

As Morpheus said to Neo in *The Matrix*, "Welcome to the real world." Left under the control of your mind's judgments and fears, the airport scene in front of you might conjure up childhood paranoia about missing out on Santa or some other big event. But that's useless information from the past. Choose not to dwell on the past.

So, stranded traveler—dance, shout, and shake your body down to the ground. You can do this. Grab your smartphone and stick it in airplane mode. Wipe the gunk off your lenses. You're on a mission. Your darling is home, heart-sick for you too. Why not photograph something that says "I love you," and text it to your someone special with an assuring note. That's love, baby. And love is mindfulness.

THE 5-4-3-2-1 TECHNIQUE

If you are ever desperate and hopeless, dial 988 (the U.S. Suicide & Crisis Lifeline). A patient and compassionate person on the other end of the phone might guide you in a grounding technique like the "5-4-3-2-1." It's downright miraculous how quickly this practice can return you to center and safety. Give it a try now.

WHAT ARE 5 THINGS YOU CAN SEE?

Simply allow your eyes be attracted to something. Blink your eyes and take a mental snapshot. Do it again, blink. Do it again, blink.

WHAT ARE 4 THINGS YOU CAN FEEL?

What's touching your skin? Feel your nose hair tickled by the breath, your tongue on your teeth, your soft dog's fur, your face in a bucket of ice.

WHAT ARE 3 THINGS YOU CAN HEAR?

Weed eater, truck noise, clicking keyboard. Sounds intensify and fade. What sounds capture your attention? How do they feel in your body?

WHAT ARE 2 THINGS YOU CAN SMELL?

Whew! Stinky armpit and stale coffee. Is that breakfast that I smell? I lost much of my sense of smell and this practice helps. How about you?

WHAT IS 1 THING YOU CAN TASTE?

Got one of those pieces of gum that makes you sneeze? Pop that into your mouth and notice the flavor. No gum? Try licking your own skin.

2. CAPTURE the present moment

- ACT OPPOSITE TO EMOTION • TURN SMARTPHONE INTO CAMERA
- PHOTOGRAPH MINDFULLY • NOTE YOUR LEVEL OF PEACE

"Capture moments, not things."

THE UNIVERSE

Imagine you just "woke up" from being mentally and emotionally hijacked. Hand on heart, you took three belly breaths and then noted your level of inner peace. You made the decision to take action and turn from useless ruminations.

ACT OPPOSITE TO YOUR EMOTIONS AND GET TO IT

This is the moment of choice. Feel the fear and do it anyway. Remember, you get to be a kid for a few minutes. Embrace your beginner's mind. Humble yourself and get curious. Like Yoda said to Luke, "You must unlearn what you have learned." In other words, "admit you don't know shit." Shift from your dark, self-limiting thoughts to the possibilities that arise from conscious presence. Let go of control and perfectionism. There is no peace there whatsoever. For the next few minutes, radically accept God's will and God's way.

Commit to being present with intrusive thoughts and unpleasant body sensations. Commit to completing the practice. You are not your thoughts. Just observe them. Feel the effects of your thoughts on your body. Resistance to the now is futile. Be brave and vulnerable.

TURN YOUR SMARTPHONE INTO A CAMERA (AIRPLANE MODE ON, WI-FI OFF)

When you set your smartphone to Airplane Mode with Wi-Fi off, it affirms your commitment to experiencing presence without interruption. For this mindful moment, your smartphone becomes just a camera. There is no need to check social media, return mom's call, catch up on political news, or reply to the boss's text that just beeped at you. Now, clean your lenses. Avoid shooting your assignment with last night's enchiladas smudged on your lens.

CAPTURE THE PRESENT MOMENT

Capturing a pretty photo and capturing the present moment are different. Of course, as you master photography, even simple snaps become more visually appealing. That's great. However, that's not the point of mindful photography. Want to grasp the spirit of mindful photography? Turn your smartphone into a camera and ask a child to take several photos of things they are most grateful

WHAT IS PHOTOGRAPHING MINDFULLY?

PHOTOGRAPHING CONSCIOUSLY	PHOTOGRAPHING UNCONSCIOUSLY
Creating for Connection	*Creating for Likes*
Focused on 5 Senses	*Detached from Reality*
Lost in Creation	*Lost in Thought*
Present	*Hurried*
Aware	*Asleep*

for. Observe them. Watch them get lost in creating, while total-ly unconcerned about perfection. Notice the "heart" in what they show you.

You have now witnessed capturing the present moment versus ego-centered photography.

Become a child and start moving. All that resistance energy is just a drain and waste. Get busy flowing in the moment with the action happening in front of your eyeballs, not your brain. That's what kids do.

Feel what's attracting you and what makes you feel good inside. Let body tingles, rather than judging thoughts, move you towards a subject. Notice what you are attracted to. Trust your gut and let your sight pull you towards things. Take time with each shot. Keep noting your level of peace and then return to the photo at hand. You may hear thoughts like, "This is useless." Come back to the photo at hand. "These photos look like crap." Come back to the photo at hand. "My job sucks." Come back to the photo at hand.

EDIT, CHOOSE & DELETE

As you edit your photos, edit for the moment you captured. Did you shoot a bunch of interesting textures? Convert those to black and white and crank up the contrast. Were you in the forest shooting fall aspen leaves? You might want to lift your shadows, darken your blacks, and warm your shots up a bit. Did you capture a portrait at the dog park of a friend with their lab? Try a shallow depth of field and a slight vignette.

Tinker. Play. Try things you've never tried. Like color filters? Make these black and white. Prefer an austere look? Try bold colors for a change.

You're not editing to "get" better at photography or to "get" likes. You lack nothing. So there's nothing to "get." You are editing for the same reason as you shoot: to capture the present moment. Get absorbed in the photos you are editing.

On a recent trip to San Antonio I went for a mindful photowalk through the grounds of the Alamo. I did a heart-check and got to it, shooting both wide and tight shots. I deleted all but the ones that made me feel good inside. Street photography is great for transcending ego and being immersed in fun energy.

As judgment and fear creep in, keep noting your level of peace and coming back to the editing at hand. Marvel at your creative gift of capturing the now. When you use your camera as an instrument of gratitude, whatever you create is a masterpiece. Pronounce your favorite few shots "finished!" and give thanks for your creative gifts. This will help affirm the healing effects of exercising your talents.

Now, it's time to get ruthless. Delete the remaining photos. That's right. Gone for good. Go to your "Deleted" folder and delete those photos permanently. You are aiming to keep a few of the most moment-capturing shots that you will preserve for future reminders of peace presence. This is part of "wanting what we have" versus "having what we want." From here forward, your photo library is going to look more like a pristine, curated gallery and less like a hoarder's reality show.

Put your culled shots in a folder and name the folder something that's meaningful to you.

Once again, take time to check your level of inner peace. Put your hand on your heart after you have made those hard decisions to tidy up. What does it feel like to declutter? How is your level of inner peace now?

Don't let go of your heart just yet. It's getting ready to guide you on your next assignment. It's time to shine your beautiful light and to feel the deep, lasting presence found in blessing others with your gifts.

3. SHINE your light on someone

• LOVE SOMEONE • STAY OFF SOCIAL MEDIA • NOTE YOUR LEVEL OF PEACE

"You are the light of the world. A town built on a hill cannot be hidden. Neither do people light a lamp and put it under a bowl. Instead they put it on its stand, and it gives light to everyone in the house. In the same way, let your light shine before others, that they may see your good deeds and glorify your Father in heaven."

MATTHEW 5, 14-16

IMAGINE SELF-IMPROVEMENT AND PROFESSIONAL DEVELOPMENT BEING SUBSTITUTED FOR THE LIFE OF SERVICE

Imagine becoming familiar with your greatest gifts and using them to bless others. We are designed to help one another. Putting a smile on the cashier's face is service. Spending time with mom is service. Helping an alcoholic find a meeting is service.

Service is love. Love puts you in the highest state of mindfulness. Love is what you are designed to do.

The third step of shining our light on someone creates the loving presence that each of us so desperately wants. This is where we truly bless someone with what we've created, without fishing for compliments.

Send mom a text and tell her that the flowers you photographed remind you of the color and love she brought into the house. Look at one of the images you created and say a silent prayer for a friend. Send your spouse a photo of the kids blowing a kiss. Send your

Howdy Mom! Saw lots of these out on the trail today. None of them are as beautiful as you! Thank you for being my mother, confidant, and cheerleader. I love you. <3

Duuude! A local bear left a little present for you today. I'll wrap it up and mail it to you for your B.S. collection! :-)) You rock. Let's talk soon.

Howdy Jon! I just want you to know how inspiring your keynote was at the conference. The group hike was really special too. Thanks for the encouraging words you shared with me. It came at just the right time. Bless you my friend.

Good morning Maria! You are making such great progress! Remember the mindful photography exercise we discussed in your session yesterday? As promised, here are some "texture" shots that I took recently. Can't wait to see yours before we meet again next week. Don't forget to breathe! =)

sweetie a photo of an old framed portrait of you two at the senior prom, and tell her she's even more beautiful now (or tell him that he's as handsome as ever). At work, use photography to shine the light on the people around you, versus yourself.

As a feeling, love is the most powerful sensation. As an act, love is the most selfless gesture. Most of the time my reactions and judgments are of a far lower vibration, but I keep trying to respond out of love. Fear makes it challenging. Love is almost like a magnet pulling us towards a person or an idea. In business and personal relationships, I seek to realize that each of us is love.

As you do acts of love, it is important to keep checking in with your body sensations.

Are you feeling tingling? Butterflies? Warmth? Are your facial muscles changing? Feeling these sensations will help you "tag" pleasant body feelings to love, and it will draw you to even more.

SERVING THROUGH PHOTOGRAPHY

Serving with your camera can take the form of a worldwide humanitarian effort side-by-side with Mother Teresa. But, it can also take the form of showing up at a family event with a camera, being the designated photographer, and preserving memories for those present.

Important: stay off social media. You will be tempted to post your creations, seeking validation. Don't get caught in that trap. You're making one-on-one, meaningful connections here. Humble, heart-felt connections.

I can serve regardless of how I feel at the moment. I am a child of God and a spiritual tuning fork of the universe. I was destined to serve. Do you think John Lennon was right when he said that the love we take is equal to the love we make?

Service is the ultimate example of acting opposite to your emotions. After all, when you feel low or anxious, the last thing you want to do is text someone a recent photo you took along with a message of encouragement. But when you focus on service, you send it anyway.

Need a little kick in the butt? Say a little prayer like "God, I am yours. I obviously have no idea what the heck I am doing. You clearly put me in a world of many people in pain. You want me to love others, they need help, so I guess it's time for me to get out of myself and get to work."

GIVE A PRINT. SHARE A STORY. MAKE SOMEONE'S DAY.

Push back against the thoughts that tell you it's no use—that it won't make you feel any better. Service to others who have similar struggles to your own is the ultimate form of mindful love. I know many people whose service work seems to come so naturally for them. For me, that's not the case. When I'm a moody mess I'd much rather isolate myself than pick up the phone and focus my attention on someone else's story. However, without fail, when I focus on others, it lessens my own preponderance of my so-called problems.

Who might need you right now? Take a silly selfie, text it to your friend with a corny joke, and make them laugh. Observe how your body reacts.

"I reckon the answer to any problem I can have is the question: "who ya helpin'?"

Anonymous

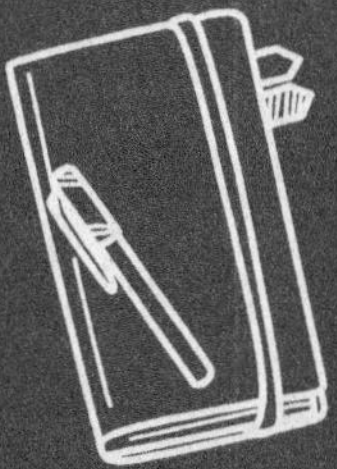

JOURNALING AND MOOD CHARTING

At the end of each practice you will find corresponding journal prompts. During your morning quiet time you might review a few photos and write in your journal about yesterday's mindful photography practice. Keep it old-school and use paper and pen versus an electronic method. Journaling with ink-on-paper will improve your results and bolster your creativity.

In fact, a University of Tokyo study revealed that writing on physical paper with its tactile experience creates more brain activity and improved memory while recalling the information an hour later.[12]

∞ *How did this practice affect your inner peace? How do you see light differently now? What came up during your shoot? Now that you've culled your photos, let go of the rest, and give them a home in your phone's photo app. Do you feel a sense of accomplishment from following through? Note that.*

∞ *Did you experience anger, joy, agitation, peace, sadness, elation, or frustration? Note that. Remember, presence is the goal of these practices, not feeling happy. Peace comes when you aren't constantly bracing against tough emotions. By doing this practice, you just took aim, trusted, and went for it. Congratulations for participating in your own healing. Keep trusting the process, not your emotions. The process yields the results, not your thinking.*

PART III

MINDFUL PHOTOGRAPHY PRACTICES

*"Before enlightenment; chop wood, carry water.
After enlightenment; chop wood, carry water."*

ZEN PROVERB

FOLLOW THE LIGHT

Observing light is a portal to mindfulness. The following three practices are effective during acute distress to turn a dark thought-spiral into peaceful presence. "Following the light" trains us to keep our face, camera, and attention pointed towards the source of light. As a result, our subject (and ourselves) come alive with a positive energy.

You walk into this scene on a sunny New England morning. It's all so beautiful—what should you photograph? Be the one out of million photographers who mindfully notices tiny details, like the way the hard backlight from the sunrise makes a humble shoreline rock come alive with sparkling light and texture.

"It's always people and light that interest me.
And when I walk down the street it's the light that I see
and not some "funny thing." If there's a reflection
or a sparkle, that's what I see and that's what I shoot."

THORSTEN OVERGAARD

In 2015 I attended a street photography workshop in New York City with Danish street photographer Thorsten Overgaard. I am grateful to have learned the "follow of the light" philosophy from him.

Thorsten is a Leica camera guy, preferring the simplified, mechanical feel of old school rangefinders. He has an avid following of Leica-minded aficionados. But I wasn't there because of any snooty camera brand. I was there because of Thorsten's YouTube channel and his beautifully simple teachings about photography (all with a way-cool Danish accent).

As my fellow workshop attendees began methodically shooting their manual-everything Leica M cameras, I proceeded to machine-gun my new full-frame Sony a7R II with snappy auto focus. I was shooting fast glass and nailing focus on subjects with incredibly shallow depth of field. Yep, I was feeling pretty good about myself among those slow-pokes.

But as that first day rolled on, I started to notice something different about Thorsten and the guys painstakingly shooting their Leicas. They were in a slowed-down state. I was exhausting myself, competing for cool shots. They were kicked back, waiting for light to unfold, and only snapping occasionally.

By day two I was in a different mindset. I slowed down and followed the light like my cohorts were doing. I didn't call it "mindful photography" back then, but that's what it felt like. Even now I can peruse the photos I shot back then and I can feel the same body sensations I felt the moment my shutter snapped.

Experiment with the following light-focused practices. As you photograph different aspects of light, observe how you begin to notice light in a new way, even without your camera. That's your attention coming back to presence.

ABOUT LIGHT

ZINC FIREWORKS REVEAL WHEN HUMAN EGG IS FERTILIZED

In a study published in Scientific Reports, Northwestern researchers discovered that when the human egg is activated by a sperm enzyme, an explosion of zinc sparks erupts.[13]

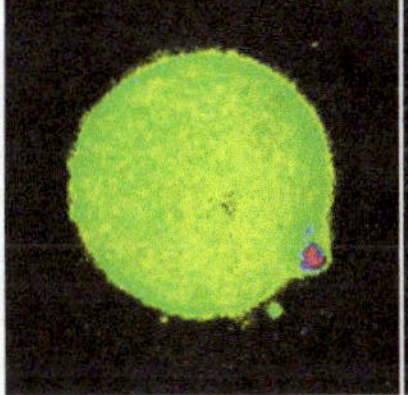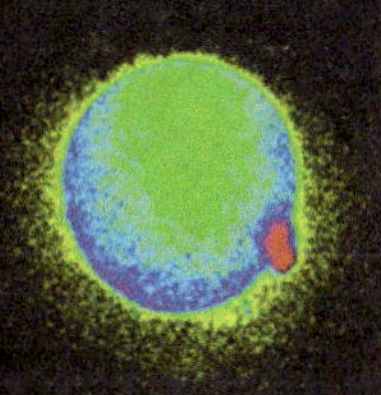

- **Light from the sun takes eight minutes to reach earth.**
- **Plato thought that we see by shooting light rays out of our eyes.**
- **A double rainbow occurs when light is reflected twice within each water droplet.**

YOUR BODY IS BIOLUMINESCENT

That's right, the human body actually emits visible light. The light can even be photographed by an ultra-sensitive camera in total darkness. This discovery was made in 2009 by a team of Japanese researchers at the Tohoku Institute of Technology.[14]

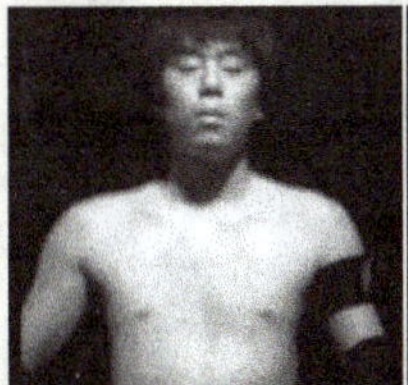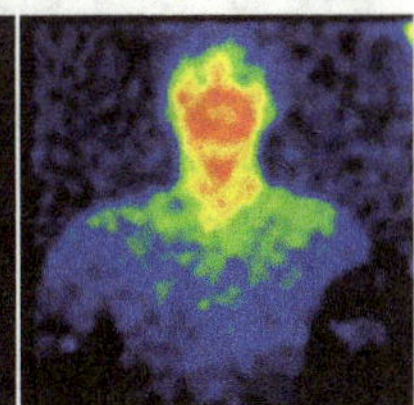

CHASE THINGS THAT SPARKLE

"The light of God surrounds us;
The love of God enfolds us;
The power of God protects us;
The presence of God watches over us;
Wherever we are, God is!"

JAMES DILLET FREEMAN

I grew up in the country in South Texas, and Saturday mornings were about cutting grass and mending fences in the heat and humidity. Years later, looking for a little sympathy, I shared that childhood memory during a marriage counseling session. The therapist flippantly remarked that I would rather be out in a field of sunflowers, chasing things that sparkled (I swear I caught my then-wife nodding).

Well my friends, join me in lifting a middle finger to the oddballs out there who would rather string barbed wire than frolic in a field of flowers. Let's take a momentary respite from the back-breaking seriousness of life and chase a few things that sparkle and fill us with joy.

During this practice you will train yourself to notice glittering flashes of light—aka sparkles. You will see common things in an inspiring way—like observing glittering gold showering down through fall Aspen trees. You will also see things you once thought were insignificant in new ways, like the twinkling highlight in your dog's eye, or the sparkle of your sweetheart's earrings.

"Who cares?" you might say. "I have a long list of grown-up problems, and childish glitters are the least of my concern."

Here is how this powerful mindfulness technique works: each time you notice a sparkle, you are turning your attention from thinking to noticing, from rumination to intense presence. Each sparkle is a beautiful interruption. Look up now and notice what sparkles at you. Stay with it for a second or two while you breathe.

Metaphorically, what is sparkling in and around you right now? Has God given you a pronounced gift that has begun to shine lately? Have you recently seen a shimmer of hope in a place where you've been stuck? Is that a tough question? I get it. When you are in an emotional malaise, everything looks monotone and blurry. Give this practice a shot and observe your present-moment absorption. You'll see light in a whole new way, including the light within yourself.

SCENARIO:

You find yourself at a holiday event downtown, filled with Christmas lights, or simply in a parking lot full of chrome and glass. Sparkles catch your attention. It's go-time.

1. FOCUS on body and surroundings

• HAND ON HEART • 3 BELLY BREATHS • NOTE YOUR LEVEL OF PEACE • OPEN YOUR EYES

With your eyes closed or gazing softly, gently place your hand on your heart and take three deep belly breaths. Simply feel your various body sensations. Note your level of inner peace. Open your eyes wide and take in what is surrounding you. Just "be" for a few seconds—without commentary or categorizations.

2. CAPTURE the present moment

• ACT OPPOSITE TO EMOTION • TURN SMARTPHONE INTO CAMERA
• PHOTOGRAPH MINDFULLY • NOTE YOUR LEVEL OF PEACE

Now, note your resistance to this practice and choose action anyway. Demonstrate your aim to experience inner peace by turning your smartphone into a camera, with airplane mode on. Wipe off your lenses, turn from useless ruminations, get off your keister, and let's have some fun. Trust me—before you know it you'll start seeing sparkles everywhere. And each time you do, you'll re-enter the now. Through your eyesight, you become engaged with your environment and disengaged from commentary.

Capture five shots of sparkles of light as they attract you. Get close. See which materials sparkle. Is it a light-source or a reflection? What angles make them sparkle most? Do a few check-ins, hand on your heart. Keep coming back to the shot at hand.

Talk about sparkles! Shooting into shimmering aspen leaves brings me joy and presence. I love to backlight and watch the sunshine shower through. It's fun to select and capture one single leaf too.

Remain present while editing, capturing the look of the moment. Delete all but a sacred few. Pronounce your collection "complete" and do another hand-on-heart check-in of your inner peace.

3. SHINE your light on someone

• LOVE SOMEONE • STAY OFF SOCIAL MEDIA • NOTE YOUR LEVEL OF PEACE

Ready to transcend the enticing familiarity of self-pity and fear? When you shine your light and bless others through mindful photography, you create the loving connections that each of us so desperately wants. You deepen your immersive photographic experience when you create images destined to touch others. Refrain from putting your mindful creations on social media for ego-validation. Instead, directly bless someone with your thing of beauty through a message or print. How can you share a photo or two with someone and make their eyes sparkle with love? Notice how you get lost in the moment when you connect with someone's heart. Do one last check-in of your inner peace with your hand over your own heart.

JOURNAL PROMPTS

∞ *What did it feel like to intentionally place your hand on your heart, taking three belly breaths?*

∞ *Describe your body sensations after acting opposite to your emotions and following through with this practice.*

∞ *Since your practice, have you begun noticing more things that sparkle in your surroundings? Describe them. How about inside yourself?*

Here's the funny thing: chase sparkles and I swear you'll start seeing them everywhere. Noticing things surrounding us is a good thing. We're spending the majority of our waking hours mindlessly ingesting screen-fed content intended to convince us of things. As you practice, you are creating your own content intended to foster peaceful presence inside you and others. As you are capturing, editing, and blessing others, keep checking in with your heart and your level of presence.

PHOTO TIP: STARBURSTS

A starburst is the result of light diffraction, or the bending of light waves around the aperture blades inside your lens. Shoot into the sunlight and let the sun "kiss" the edge of an object. Play with it. Tweak the angle, bend the light, get funky.

FACE TOWARDS THE SUNSHINE

*"Keep your face always towards the sunshine,
and the shadows will fall behind you."*

M. B. WHITMAN, 1903

This is going to sound like a cheesy entry in a J. Peterman catalog, but it actually happened to me in my mid-20s. I was on a solo trip in Guatemala, and I decided to travel to the eastern jungles to explore the ruins of Tikal. I was to be there for three nights, sleeping in a hammock slung under a palapa beside some fellow sojourners. In my backpack were a few new paperbacks, including Norman Vincent Peale's, *The Power of Positive Thinking*.

As a little background, I was raised to believe in Jesus as a Savior, part of a God who loved me personally. But I was a mischievous rascal at times, and that lifestyle wasn't blending well with biblical teachings. My relationship with God had become strained, and I was lost.

Fast forward to that jungle palapa when I cracked open Reverend Peale's famous book. I read about the transformative power of positive thoughts. There were teachings on holding a mental picture of myself succeeding, never permitting it to fade. He explained how our minds seek to develop the photos we hold in our imagination. Today these ideas are old hat, but at the time I was set on fire. I was feeling the presence of God's positive, electrifying spirit. Negativity and self-condemnation never really motivated lasting change for me. I started memorizing positive, affirming scriptures, and my outlook on God changed.

Choosing the positive is a lifelong challenge. Perhaps you are like me: I can start chewing on my past and sometimes, like cotton

candy, it tastes mighty good. I mean, what can be more stimulating than critiquing and redesigning my past? It absorbs my attention and, for a few moments at least, makes me think I'm actually affecting something. Unfortunately, like cotton candy, once the buzz wears off, I end up feeling empty.

So join me in some mindful positivity. Let's develop a reflex to turn towards the presence of light in times of distress, rather than trying to figure things out.

You will be practicing the magic of backlighting—simply putting your subject between you and the sun. Your photos will begin to sparkle in a frame of light. Regardless of the scene—from mountain vistas to bowls of bananas—your snaps will begin to dazzle and inspire your attention.

To contrast "keeping your face towards the sunshine," you'll also turn towards shadows as your thoughts are constantly doing. You'll create beautiful images while focusing on the play of light and shadows. When you voluntarily choose non-judgmental presence with the dark areas of yourself, you become free, and the present starts to feel less burdensome.

You will continue to master photographic techniques. But most importantly, you'll experience the presence that comes from having your senses fixed on beautiful light and the unburdened present moment.

SCENARIO:

You're with a friend on a sunny late-afternoon walk without a cloud in the sky. You look down to shield your eyes from the glare of the harsh sun. In doing so, you see hard shadows on the sidewalk. Glancing at your friend, you know what to do. Time to practice backlighting.

1. FOCUS on body and surroundings

• **HAND ON HEART** • **3 BELLY BREATHS** • **NOTE YOUR LEVEL OF PEACE**
• **OPEN YOUR EYES**

With your eyes closed or gazing softly, gently place your hand on your heart and take three deep belly breaths. Simply feel your various body sensations. Note your level of inner peace. Feel the sunshine. Open your eyes wide and take in what is surrounding you. Just "be" for a few seconds—without commentary or categorizations.

2. CAPTURE the present moment

• **ACT OPPOSITE TO EMOTION** • **TURN SMARTPHONE INTO CAMERA**
• **PHOTOGRAPH MINDFULLY** • **NOTE YOUR LEVEL OF PEACE**

Note your resistance to this practice and choose action anyway. Demonstrate your aim to experience inner peace by turning your smartphone into a camera, with airplane mode on. Wipe off your lenses and get your body to the best place to capture a few mindful shots.

Backlighting is magic—and it's simple. Put your subject between you and the sun. Shoot up through pine needles with sunlight sparkling through. Photograph your animal friend with the bedside lamp directly behind. Backlight a person so that the sun forms a rim around their hair and shoulders. Grab a sheet of paper and bounce light back into their face. Imagine yourself blessing your subject by your presence.

Now, check out the shadows cast by the powerful light of the sun. Snap the shadow of a walker on the bright concrete. Experiment photographing the hard shadows of flowers, removing color as the allure. Notice hard shadows and soft shadows.

You can see beauty in the shadows if you choose that perspective. Can you embrace your present shadows as part of the human experience? Can you see the inseparable mixture of light and shadow, joy and sadness? The presence of God is everywhere, even in those places that are hard to accept.

Remain present while editing, capturing the look of the moment. Were you capturing shadows? How about converting to black and white? Try adjusting your black point and shadow sliders until the shadow becomes the most prominent part of the photo. Are you editing a back-lit portrait? Try raising your shadows a bit. Try a light vignette. Notice how you can get lost in the present moment while editing.

Delete all but a sacred few. Pronounce your collection "complete" and do another hand-on-heart check-in of your inner peace.

In hard-light environments, shooting in black and white and cranking up the contrast is a great way to notice the interplay between dark and light. Take a moment, squint your eyes just a little, and focus on the shadows in these shots. Just notice the shapes created by the dark areas. Now, do the same with the highlights. Focus intensely. What shapes do you see? Your mind has an amazing capacity to change perspective if you will it to. Ask yourself, "What is the darkest, heaviest concern on my mind right now?" And finally, "How can I flip this mental fixation and focus, even for a moment, on the brightness in the picture instead?"

3. SHINE your light on someone

• LOVE SOMEONE • STAY OFF SOCIAL MEDIA • NOTE YOUR LEVEL OF PEACE

Ready to transcend the enticing familiarity of self-pity and fear? When you shine your light and bless others through mindful photography, you create the loving connections that each of us so desperately wants. You deepen your immersive photographic experience when you create images destined to touch others. Refrain from putting your mindful creations on social media for ego-validation. Instead, directly bless someone with your thing of beauty through a message or print. How can you share a photo or two with someone that makes them notice the warm sunshine in their face? What about sending a trusted friend a note about what mindful photography is teaching you about yourself. Notice how you get lost in the moment when you connect with someone's heart. Do one last check-in of your inner peace with your hand over your own heart.

JOURNAL PROMPTS

∞ *Describe any resistance you noticed when turning from negative thoughts and instead focusing your attention towards the light. How did you push through?*

∞ *What shift in mindset happened when you cut off your internet connection and turned your smartphone into a camera?*

∞ *Were you tempted to share your creation on social media? What are your thoughts on using your photos to bless one single person instead of posting publicly?*

PHOTO TIP: DYNAMIC RANGE

In the evolution of photography, the dynamic range of an image from lightest to darkest has come a long way. Think of film. If you photographed Aunt Gertrude in front of a sunny window, you might need a bright flash to expose her jolly face. Nowadays, digital cameras do an amazing job of keeping image detail, even in a scene with the brightest of highlights and the darkest of shadows. Smartphones, using HDR (High Dynamic Range) software, often beat out high-end dedicated digital cameras in their ability to handle previously impossible shots, like these "Face Towards the Sunshine" practices.

However, physics still has its limits. Check out the two photos above, shot with the same iPhone. It was late evening when I snapped the top one, and the shadows came out pure black. The tiny smartphone sensor needed more light to properly expose the shot, and instead created a silhouette. The next shot, taken at a brighter time of day, shows plenty of highlight and shadow details, straight out of camera.

andcr   Doug
Sweet
NDE

NO MATCHY, NO MATCHY

"The artwork doesn't have to match the sofa."

GOD

For me, college was a struggle. My emotional challenges were getting worse, and the partying was out of control. When I look back at those years, I remember two sanctuaries from the storm. The first was a small chapel on campus. I made quite a few entries in the big prayer book that was front and center of the dimly lit room filled with traditional pews and flipped-down kneelers.

The other place was the art building. I got lost in my presence there. That place dismantled me as an artist. My tight style from high school painting class was shamed away, and I was off to the races, splashing conceptual pop crap around that never found a permanent place on the wall after dorm years.

But there was one classroom in that building where the visual aesthetic was still sacred. Elizabeth Ridenhaur, I still think of you. Elizabeth was a trip. Long legged, she wore a super-wide belt and big black glasses, and she spoke with wide hand gestures. "No matchy! No matchy!" she often said.

An example of "no matchy" would be my old college buddy Andrew. He amassed a treasure-trove of daddy-o thrift store clothes, and possessed an "I got dressed in the dark" vibe. He called it the "uncaring look," and he pulled it off like a boss.

(left) Horsing around with my son Caleb. When I first got that down jacket it drove me nuts trying to wear things that matched it. The neon green attracted comments like: "Sale rack?"

So, you with the beige pants and subtle heather shirt—don a green sombrero and an orange grass skirt and let's think of color in a whole new way.

SCENARIO:

You know you are a creative person. You pride yourself in things looking "just right." You've always gotten ego-satisfying compliments on just how darned put-together you always look. So, what's the problem? Well, your "good taste" has turned into a bunch of limiting rules that are holding you back from imagining new possibilities.

1. FOCUS on body and surroundings

• HAND ON HEART • 3 BELLY BREATHS • NOTE YOUR LEVEL OF PEACE • OPEN YOUR EYES

With your eyes closed or gazing softly, gently place your hand on your heart and take three deep belly breaths. Simply feel your various body sensations. Note your level of inner peace. Open your eyes wide and take in what is surrounding you. Just "be" for a few seconds—without commentary or categorizations.

2. CAPTURE the present moment

• ACT OPPOSITE TO EMOTION • TURN SMARTPHONE INTO CAMERA • PHOTOGRAPH MINDFULLY • NOTE YOUR LEVEL OF PEACE

Ready to get your freak on? Note your resistance to this silly practice and choose action anyway. Demonstrate your aim to experience inner peace by turning your smartphone into a camera, with airplane mode on. Wipe off your lenses and let's notice how color affects us.

Dig into the back of your dresser, rifle through your closet, and grab an outfit or two that hideously does not match. Think: Cindy Lauper, early 80s. Take a few photos of those cringe-worthy color combos. Feel how your body responds to color. Snap that pink tutu on a toy poodle against granny's sable coat. Take some risks and break some color rules.

Now, go out into nature and photograph things that do not match. Judge the heck out of them too. Expose how much that purple flower clashes next to the blue-green grass. Notice how ugly that red berry is in the brown mud below. Look at that atrocious bird wearing blue, white, and black—doesn't he know that went out of style years ago?

Do you get where I'm going with this? In truth, the Creator didn't create color-rules for nature. Notice how all colors and tones and shades fit together in God's world.

Now my friend, go forth and shoot. Start to ponder how color affects you. Notice the rules you create around color. Are any of your "creative rules" actually serving to hold you back? Photograph things that go together and things that don't. Then, ask yourself "Why?"

Remain present while editing, capturing the look of the moment. Oversaturate your colors. Crank up the contrast. Get funky. Delete all but a sacred few. Pronounce your collection "complete" and do another hand-on-heart check-in of your inner peace.

3. SHINE your light on someone

• LOVE SOMEONE • STAY OFF SOCIAL MEDIA • NOTE YOUR LEVEL OF PEACE

Ready to transcend the enticing familiarity of self-pity and fear? When you shine your light and bless others through mindful photography, you create the loving connections that each of us so desperately wants. You deepen your immersive photographic experience when you create images destined to touch others. Refrain from putting your mindful creations on social media for ego-validation. Instead, directly bless someone with your thing of beauty through a message or print. Who do you know that could use a good laugh? Well, send them a photo of your poodle wearing a pink skirt and a black top-hat. Go for it. Shoot them a note too, exclaiming "No matchy!" Notice how you get lost in the moment when you connect with someone's heart. Do one last check-in of your inner peace with your hand over your own heart.

JOURNAL PROMPTS

∞ *Does the idea of wearing clothes that don't match make you cringe? When did you pick up those rules?*

∞ *Were you able to photograph any colors in nature that don't match? Why is this a trick question?*

∞ *What benefits come from remaining in self-pity and fear? Can a selfless gesture bring love to dark thought patterns? Why?*

Dad took "no matchy" to a whole new level. Color-blind and a golfer to boot, his outfits usually needed sanctioning by Mom before heading out the door.

Take a little walk around your neighborhood and find some funky color combinations, like these in Glenwood Springs, Colorado.

TV
Mail

FOSTER GRATITUDE

If you find yourself trapped in a state of lack, these practices will help you find lasting freedom. Gratitude is a portal to inner peace. Practicing gratitude is a reliable way to enter a mindful state in the here and now. This tool is available to you at all waking moments. A grateful state is a mindful state. These mindful photography exercises will immediately elevate you to a higher plane. And the great thing is, you don't have to "get" anything to reach it.

"The moment you begin to worry about the things you want and the things you don't have in life is the moment you lose your gratitude."

Zig Ziglar

Most people agree that gratitude is a good thing. But gratitude doesn't come naturally, does it? When I'm in an emotional crisis, my last instinct is to find a pen and scribble the names of three people I love on the palm of my hand. However, I have learned from years of experience that intervening techniques like this always do the trick. Try it now. A humble and determined act like this will not go unnoticed by God. Place that written-on hand upon your heart for a few moments, even if you don't feel like it. Note. Observe. Make it a game.

To reap the full rewards of a gratitude practice, let's try to understand what gratitude really is.

Imagine yourself having your morning quiet time with your journal open in front of you. You woke up grouchy and are trying to compensate with coffee. Pondering your day ahead makes you feel like an anxious mess. You muster up just enough determination to grab your pen and scratch out three things you are grateful for: "coffee, paycheck, Suzie."

Now, completely transformed, you relax into your morning chair, bathing in a warm glow of gratitude. All good, right? Hardly. In fact, I frequently hear this while talking to friends on their own faith journey: "I get started with a daily morning gratitude list, but I just keep listing the same things over and over, and then I quit doing it."

A mindful approach to gratitude might be in order. I can look over at my Snoopy coffee mug right now and say out loud or to myself, "I'm grateful for coffee!" While there might be some value in that, let's try an approach that goes much deeper.

I take a fresh glance back at my Snoopy coffee mug. I raise my smartphone and capture a mindful photo, then set that aside. Now, I allow impressions to emerge. My mother, now with the Lord, sent me this mug for Christmas a few years back, and it means a lot to me. Rather than going into a long story in my mind, I just sit with what my mom's spirit means to me, feeling the body sensations deep inside. I write

down "Mom" and send her a prayer. My mind then drifts to the coffee itself. An image emerges in my head of the Ethiopian man who harvested these coffee beans. I picture him with his family and bless him as I write down "Ethiopian & family."

I do a heart-check and feel the spirit of gratitude inside me growing.

This full-body approach to fostering gratitude helps when you need to get your attitude back on track. The key component is connecting gratitude-producing action to good feelings in the body. Physical sensations always accompany gratitude. Experiment. Notice your facial muscles. Any tingles in your belly area? What is your breath doing? Before long, you'll start searching for good and lasting things that come from love and gratitude.

Trust in the process of these practices, and keep proving the results to yourself. Keep doing hand-on-heart check-ins. Notice your level of presence. Don't take anyone else's word for what works and what doesn't. Trust your own body feelings and let gratitude lead you to the truth. Are you having problems in your marriage? Practice gratitude. Facing uncertainty at work? Lean into gratitude even more. Notice miracles, bless others, and let a grateful heart transform your life.

GRATITUDE—TEXTING VS POSTING

Do the effects of sharing gratitude differ when it is expressed one-to-one privately via text, or shared publicly online?

Numerous investigations to date have established the benefits of expressing gratitude for improved psychological well-being and interpersonal relationships. Nevertheless, the social dynamics of gratitude remain understudied. Overall, participants assigned to any digital gratitude intervention experienced improvements in gratitude, positive emotions, negative emotions, elevation, connectedness, support, and loneliness.[15]

Relative to all other conditions, participants assigned to text their benefactors showed the biggest boosts in social connectedness and support.

BEAUTY IN UNCERTAINTY

"Take courage my heart
Stay steadfast my soul
He's in the waiting
He's in the waiting

Hold onto your hope
As your triumph unfolds
He's never failing
He's never failing"

"TAKE COURAGE"
SONG BY KRISTENE DIMARCO

If you are in the midst of change that is overwhelming you and stealing your joy, this practice is for you.

In mindful photography, you capture the present moment with each press of the shutter button. There is no uncertainty in the present moment. Rather, uncertainty arises while you are lost in thought, trying to escape the unpleasant body sensations that come with fretting and controlling. You cast uncertainty into your past through regret. You project uncertainty into your future through worry.

So, what's the solution? Sojourners, if we are to escape the hell of habitual depression and anxiety, we have but one choice: find the beauty in this moment, this one day, with whatever it brings. We must get this "be-here-now" business, or we'll be self-condemned to a life in fear of uncertainty.

Are you willing to use your smartphone camera and photo app to expose and face your uncertainty? Take courage—you are not reaching higher by yourself. I and many others are with you in spirit and fully understand how you feel. These practices work. Trust in the process. The Spirit is with you too, comforting you, guiding you, and loving you during these mindful photography moments. You'll experience a time-transcending sweetness through creativity. Nothing is more authentic than expressing your devotion to recovery by facing the primal fear of your life's uncertainties.

In the realm of the Spirit, there is freedom and expansion and breakthrough. If we put limits on God, we will miss the transformation that comes from loosening our grip on plans and courageously facing uncertainty.

SCENARIO:

There is that feeling in your gut again. Love has a distinct feeling. Anger has a distinct feeling. But this? This is the unmistakable feeling of uncertainty usually associated with the question: "What the hell is going to become of me?"

1. FOCUS on body and surroundings

• HAND ON HEART • 3 BELLY BREATHS • NOTE YOUR LEVEL OF PEACE • OPEN YOUR EYES

With your eyes closed or gazing softly, gently place your hand on your heart and take three deep belly breaths. Simply feel your various body sensations. Note your level of inner peace. Open your eyes wide and take in what is surrounding you. Just "be" for a few seconds without commentary or categorizations.

Let your body be drawn to an image in front of you that typifies the uncertainty you are experiencing right now. Your front door knob might represent this place you will soon miss because of an upcoming relocation. A debit card sticking out of your wallet might represent financial uncertainty. A half-gallon of ice cream might represent you not knowing whether you are going to polish the whole thing off tonight watching Seinfeld reruns.

2. CAPTURE the present moment

• ACT OPPOSITE TO EMOTION • TURN SMARTPHONE INTO CAMERA
• PHOTOGRAPH MINDFULLY • NOTE YOUR LEVEL OF PEACE

Note your resistance to this practice and choose action anyway. Demonstrate your aim to experience inner peace by turning your smartphone into a camera, with airplane mode on. Wipe off your lenses, turn from useless ruminations, get off your keister, and let's have some fun. Soon you will start intuitively seeing beauty in uncertainty. And each time you do, you'll re-enter the now. Through your eyesight, you become engaged with your environment and disengaged from commentary.

Your door knob shot was cool, with the whole living room reflected in the shiny brass. You rotated your wallet around just so, and caught beautiful highlights on the edges of those debit cards. As for the ice cream carton—well, you got such a sugar buzz that you completely forgot to shoot that. But, you did get a shot of the chocolate that dripped on your belly. All good.

Intent on reducing your final shots to just three, you blessed the duds and emptied the trash. You tucked the keepers into a folder in your photos app and pronounced your collection "done." As you checked in with yourself again, you could feel those lovely muscles in your cheeks. You were smiling.

3. SHINE your light on someone

• LOVE SOMEONE • STAY OFF SOCIAL MEDIA • NOTE YOUR LEVEL OF PEACE

Ready to transcend the enticing familiarity of self-pity and fear? When you shine your light and bless others through mindful photography, you create the loving connections that each of us so desperately wants. Refrain from putting your mindful creations on social media for ego-validation. Instead, directly bless someone with your thing of beauty through a message or print.

In this case, you figure that your girlfriend won't be too impressed by photos of a doorknob, the edges of debit cards, and a chocolate-stained shirt. You opt to send your mindful creations to your life-coach instead, as they will be good thought-starters during your next session.

Do one last check-in of your inner peace with your hand over your own heart.

JOURNAL PROMPTS

∞ *What shift in mindset happened when you cut off your internet connection and turned your smartphone into a camera?*

∞ *What sort of shots represented your uncertainty? What was it like to not avoid those physical representations of your fear?*

∞ *In making a true connection with another person with one of your mindful photos, what did you experience? Detail the body sensations you felt, and whether, even if temporarily, you felt peace in uncertainty.*

Objects around us can come to represent thoughts, and those thoughts can produce unpleasant body sensations from past trauma. Through mindful photography we can beautifully portray these things, turning them into simple form. Stripping the narrative away and focusing on creative composition can permanently transform triggers into benign objects of beauty. Remember, as you are capturing, editing, and blessing yourself, keep breathing into your heart.

PHOTO TIP: BREATHING WITH YOUR CAMERA

Just like a sharpshooter practicing critical breathing techniques, we camera warriors must learn to bring our breath into the rhythm of each shot. You might find it steady and mindful to press the shutter while slowly exhaling, or at the bottom of the breath. Breath awareness is also great for getting "unstuck" in the middle of a practice. When in doubt about what to shoot, take a few belly breaths and watch the subject appear.

NOTICE MIRACLES

"I believe in miracles
Where you from
You sexy thing?

I believe in miracles
Since you came along
You sexy thing"

"You Sexy Thing"
Song by Hot Chocolate

Some years back, a painful, rapidly-growing cancerous bump formed on top of my left ear. A surgeon did an amazing job of cutting off the top of my ear and then performing restorative surgery. That ear looks slightly funky now, but I'm so grateful that it was saved. Now that's a miracle worth photographing!

As you engage in this practice, pay special attention to the body sensations you experience as you photograph objects or scenes that represent miracles to you. If you really get vulnerable and let yourself "go there" emotionally, you're going to tap into some powerful tinglings and yearnings. Feel that. Ride the range of pleasant and not-so-pleasant emotions.

Of course, miracles can be a mixed bag. God brought about a new job, but only after the other previous-miracle job ended. God brought about a new romantic love in my life, but that was after the loss of the previous-miracle one. Get where I'm going with that?

But there is another sort of miracle that I'm 100% certain your God has manifested into your life. It wasn't a new hotty, another zero at the end of your bank balance, or even the miracle of a healed child. Looking back, can you see what the suffering brought you? Things like greater love, patience, willingness, honesty, and compassion?

So, by all means, shoot some things that are physical miracles and manifestations. Lord knows we all need them as physical reminders that our prayers are heard. But in addition to that, mindfully take a few snaps of transcendent things that represent the only thing that lasts, which is love.

SCENARIO:

Your gratitude tank is low. You're caught in the rut of routine. You find yourself begging God for some miracle to happen out there, somewhere, in the abstract future.

1. FOCUS on body and surroundings

- HAND ON HEART • 3 BELLY BREATHS • NOTE YOUR LEVEL OF PEACE
- OPEN YOUR EYES

With your eyes closed or gazing softly, gently place your hand on your heart and take three deep belly breaths. Simply feel your various body sensations. Note your level of inner peace. Open your eyes wide and take in what is surrounding you. Just "be" for a few seconds without commentary or categorizations.

Let your attention lightly scan around to an image in front of you that represents a miracle, great or small. I just did this myself, gazing at Frankie the Doodle, then my coffee, then my iPhone. My eyes then looked up and landed on the miracle. It was these very words on the screen in front of me, expanding with each keystroke. Through my life's challenges, my Higher Power has given me a gift to share with you.

2. CAPTURE the present moment

**• ACT OPPOSITE TO EMOTION • TURN SMARTPHONE INTO CAMERA
• PHOTOGRAPH MINDFULLY • NOTE YOUR LEVEL OF PEACE**

Note your resistance to this practice and choose action anyway. Demonstrate your aim to experience inner peace by turning your smartphone into a camera, with airplane mode on. Now, wipe off your lenses and get your body to the best place to capture a few mindful shots.

As you walk, let your inner being direct you to the miracles all around you. Shoot that bunch of dead-looking late-winter twigs that will grow dense with leaves and bright flowers in late spring. Do you walk and talk to God? Think of what a miracle that is. Walk fast and shoot a hilarious side-selfie showing you dramatically talking to thin air. On your next video call, do a screenshot and marvel at the miracle of being able to connect with people far away.

Remain present while editing, capturing the look of the moment. Delete all but a few sacred photos. Pronounce your collection "complete" and do another hand-on-heart check-in of your inner peace.

3. SHINE your light on someone

• LOVE SOMEONE • STAY OFF SOCIAL MEDIA • NOTE YOUR LEVEL OF PEACE

Ready to transcend the enticing familiarity of self-pity and fear? Shine your light and bless others through your mindful photos. You'll create loving connections and redirect your attention to the eternal. Refrain from sharing your creations on social media. Instead, bless someone directly with your photos. Notice how you get lost in the moment when you connect with someone's heart.

Imagine noticing a coworker doing something they are great at. With your undeniable charm, you convince them to let you take a few snaps. You shake your hips, get them laughing, and take a few shots. You pick the best one and do a cool edit, projecting good vibes and blessings on your friend. Behold. What is in front of you is going to bless someone and reflect God's beautiful light. Send that shot to your boss and tell him about your amazing coworker. Put this coworker in the next newsletter. Most importantly, tell him what he means to you. That's light, and light is love. You just shined your light on someone. Feels mighty good, doesn't it?

With your hand on your heart, do one last check-in of your inner peace.

JOURNAL PROMPTS

∞ *Which of your shots brought you into grateful presence the most? What was that experience like?*

∞ *What does it feel like to pare your photos down to a precious few, filed away for a future visual gratitude meditation?*

∞ *How does it feel to use photography to lift up someone else?*

Noticing miracles can change your perception of the world. Whether it's a fat puppy in your child's arms or a pine cone basking in sun, miracles respond to being recognized and begin showing up everywhere.

PHOTO TIP: NEVER SAY SMILE

Do you wonder why you have 3000 photos of your kids bearing their teeth like monkeys instead of smiling authentically? The answer is simple: "Smile!" Or, "cheese!"

Never, ever ask your subject to smile. Instead, tell them to move their body, and be willing to act like a clown. Sometimes I'll loosen people up saying, "Don't smile!" Then I'll say, "Now, lets move those hips!" Meanwhile, I'll start doing some ridiculous gyrations with my own hips, keeping my camera on burst mode, ready to catch people's reactions. Provoke authentic, endearing expressions from people. Shake your butt. Shake your boobs. Work for the shot.

THE THREE (PHOTO) BLESSINGS

*"Fix your thoughts on what is true, and honorable,
and right, and pure, and lovely, and admirable.
Think about things that are excellent and worthy of praise,
and the God of peace shall be with you."*

THE APOSTLE PAUL, WHILE IMPRISONED BY ROME

BEHOLD, THE MINDFUL PHOTOGRAPHY VERSION OF THE PROVEN "THREE BLESSINGS" PRACTICE

Also known as "Three Good Things," this is one of the most well-known positive psychology interventions. The method was created by psychologist Martin Seligman, often called the "father of positive psychology." As demonstrated by clinical research at the Duke University Health System, Three Good Things has been scientifically demonstrated to address emotional exhaustion and provide a sense of wellbeing. Some studies have shown this bedtime practice to be more effective than widely used antidepressants like SSRIs (selective serotonin reuptake inhibitors).[16]

Here's how it works: For a week, before bed, think of three good things that happened that day and write them down. Super important: write *why* each good thing happened. Through mindful photography, we are going to super-charge the effect of this exercise by attaching the psychological and spiritual power of an image to each "good thing" you list.

(left) I took my favorite local drive and, thanks to my initiative to get off the couch, my soul felt lightened. I made a pot of tasty evening tea. Good thing I paid the gas bill. I snuggled with my comfy blanket because I was able to purchase it and then I took care of it.

Unfortunately, humans gravitate towards negative thinking and negative bias. At times you may feel like you are in a constant state of comparison and judgment. Whether you see this polluted thinking as originating from the Garden of Eden or simply from an outdated instinct to propagate our own DNA, it seems to be innate to all of humankind. How can there be hope of having a half-full mindset if you have this powerful negative bias that fuels anxiety, depression, and suffering?

CHOOSE HOPE

Just as light always overcomes the dark, you can learn to purposefully re-direct your thoughts towards positive energy. Affirm that you actually *want* to break the cycle of negativity. As you take action to harness this powerful, restorative effect, you can ask your Higher Power for fortitude and breakthrough over the next week of practice.

Prepare to witness a quick change in your level of peace and presence. After beginning this practice, I started taking snaps during the day, anticipating the bedtime review. There I was, looking for the good and capturing those moments in creative ways. As I kept doing this practice, I noticed as the highlights were arising during my days. I tried to slow down and note them, sometimes capturing the scene with another photograph, tucked away for later.

The thoughts you entertain before sleep stay in your memories longer. The Three Blessings practice is God's little pre-sleep conditioner. In fact, research shows that recognizing things you are grateful for helps you relax and sleep better too.[17]

Ready to feel a peaceful sensation in your body, compounded by your visual sense? Take a risk. Abandon yourself to this practice for a week, and see if it turns into two. The results might surprise you.

THE THREE PHOTO BLESSINGS PRACTICE

For one week, before bed, think of three good things that happened that day.

As you review the positive happenings of the day, don't analyze. Simply feel your pleasant body sensations. I let my attention gently fall on impression by impression, breathing gratitude and enjoying the good sensations deep inside. The other day I noted a breakthrough on a video project I was struggling with and finally completed. I recently listed an emotional outpouring I had in prayer, and gratitude for being able to talk in a personal way to the Holy Spirit like that. Another time, even though it felt both positive and painful, I noted an opportunity God gave me to bless an unfortunate man at a McDonald's.

1. WRITE DOWN YOUR THREE POSITIVE THINGS

I have a spread in my journal with "Three Photo Blessings" up top. On the left page are seven days, each with three blessings. Over on the right page is room for the "Reflect" step to follow. So for instance, before lights-out I might list "video project breakthrough," "talk to Holy Spirit," and "man at McDonald's."

2. REFLECT ON WHY EACH GOOD THING HAPPENED

Determining the "why" of the feel-good event is the most important part of the exercise. Night after night, answering the "why" question will guide you to stand on dependable principles that will lead you "beside still waters," as the Psalm goes. Let's take the example of my video project breakthrough. I can't overstate how stressed out I was earlier that day, exhausted but committed to a deadline. I remembered how much I had been comparing myself to others. But, somehow I persevered.

Moving to the right side of my list, I thought a little deeper about the video project and jotted down a few words. It occurred to me that my project came to fruition because I persevered in the face of wanting to make an excuse and put it off for another day. This felt empowering and gave me courage for an upcoming project. I was able to produce something really cool because of thousands of hours of dedication to my trade. This reminded me that I have rare and marketable skills. Finally, I was only working on that particular video because of a series of miracles that led me to that moment here where I live—miracles that occurred amidst frightening uncertainty. I reflected on the truth that God, although usually later than I prefer, always works things together for my good.

3. CAPTURE AN IMAGE FOR EACH

Turning to my smartphone, I find an image for each thing I wrote. I keep it quick, only seeking to find a representative image. For my video project breakthrough, I took a screenshot of a cool frame in my video. To represent my powerful experience in prayer, I snapped a photo of my knees. For the McDonald's image, I took a shot of a nearby gold-ish belt that could be construed as a golden arch.

SCENARIO:

You are up for a mindful photography challenge, eager to invest time in the most impactful of all human attitudes: gratitude.

1. FOCUS on body and surroundings

- **HAND ON HEART** • **3 BELLY BREATHS** • **NOTE YOUR LEVEL OF PEACE**
- **OPEN YOUR EYES**

This practice is done for a week or two at bedtime. It's a quick and pleasurable practice each night, and just like all things of lasting value, it takes commitment. While you journey through, keep bringing your attention to body sensations as they are right now.

2. CAPTURE the present moment

- **ACT OPPOSITE TO EMOTION** • **TURN SMARTPHONE INTO CAMERA**
- **PHOTOGRAPH MINDFULLY** • **NOTE YOUR LEVEL OF PEACE**

Note your resistance to each night's practice and take action anyway. Trust that your resolve to follow your Three Photo Blessings steps around bedtime will yield inner peace. When it comes to taking photos that match your blessings, you may start noticing blessings during the day and taking photos as you go to reflect on later before sleep. That's fantastic. Let your journal entries be your testimonies to the goodness of God.

3. SHINE your light on someone

- **LOVE SOMEONE** • **STAY OFF SOCIAL MEDIA** • **NOTE YOUR LEVEL OF PEACE**

With this private practice, you don't send your images or journal entries to anyone. Let the "shine your light" action of love be towards yourself. Pray blessings over the images you have chosen, feeling their effect inside you. Notice how you get lost in the moment when you connect with your heart. Do one last check-in of your inner peace.

JOURNAL PROMPTS

∞ *What are a few things that help you stay on track with a commitment?*

∞ *As you started to string together consecutive nights, how did it feel inside?*

∞ *What body sensations do you feel while praying blessings over each night's photos? How is presence creating breakthroughs for you now?*

As you get into the habit of doing the Three Photo Blessings at bedtime, you'll start noticing things during the course of each day that you want to capture and savor for later. This was shot through my windshield while parked, during a moment of gratitude for the hot springs pool on a wintry night.

One night I was looking for a blessing, and it dawned on me that I was grateful for even learning about The Three Blessings to begin with. Next to me was the flyer created by a colleague at work, so I photographed that. Then I thought of my sister and life coach Sara, so I did a screen shot of her recent encouraging message to me. As I clicked the buttons for the screen shot, it reminded me that my hands come in mighty handy throughout the day. I thanked God for giving me strong and functional hands that allow me to help others.

PHOTO TIP: USE YOUR RAS

The Reticular Activating System (RAS) is a bundle of nerves at our brain stem that filters out unnecessary information. Through our senses, our brains receive a massive flood of information. The RAS governs that flow, and helps us notice the important things, like our name being called out in a loud crowd of people. In Mindful Photography practices, we go out looking for certain things, they show up, and we capture images of them. The mind works in much the same way. Whatever ideas we are consciously focusing on, the RAS directs our attention to those things throughout the day. Prove it to yourself. As you take photos of the blessings in your life, observe how many more show up.

Imagine you are a hummingbird with a teeny-tiny camera, able to zip to any spot in this scene. You found some tasty flowers here and you want to go back and show your friends some photos. What would you capture to give them a complete look?

SHOW STORIES

Just like all mindful photography practices, the following are designed to help you experience inner peace. Unlike some of our practices so far, some of these teachings may lead you into serious subject matter, like the destructive stories we tell ourselves. You'll learn about *showing* stories rather than *telling* them, the difference between these two ways of experiencing the world, and how to discern helpful from harmful inner dialogue. Finally, you will have fun capturing images representing a broader view of your reality, feeling the hope of divinely-inspired possibilities.

"Pleased to meet you
Hope you guess my name
But what's puzzling you
Is the nature of my game"

"Sympathy For The Devil" by The Rolling Stones

I'd like to introduce you to a contemporary author who is the most prolific storyteller of all time. Unfortunately, the author hasn't capitalized on this lifetime of work. This writer is known for spontaneously spinning dramatic tales of past and future life. Even though these stories bear little resemblance to reality, the fantasies are so engaging that people lose themselves in their drama, believing them without question. The hero of these stories has little confidence and rarely slays dragons. And the damnedest thing is, as the author keeps cranking out disappointing stories, the audience buys them up, complicit in the ever-repeating plot.

So, who is this villain of the literary world? Yep, you guessed it. The author is you.

THE STORYTELLING MIND

A while back, the Doodle and I camped at Colorado National Monument, near the Utah border. This area is like a mini-Grand Canyon, but without the crowds. It was off-season, and something about being in that isolated canyon with vast amounts of open space caused my inner dialogue to become more noticeable. In fact, on our last day there, I vlogged about it in a video entitled "Thoughts are Sentences."

Fast forward to recent times when I became particularly interested in this idea of the Storytelling Mind. It dawned on me that when strung together, the "sentences" I referred to in my vlog became a story. Mind you, these stories are rarely literary works

STORIES FROM YOUR HIGHER SELF	STORIES FROM YOUR LOWER SELF
Loving	*Fearful*
Empowering	*Depleting*
God-glorifying	*Self-glorifying*
Redemptive	*Shame-attacking*
Peaceful	*Anxiety-provoking*
Joyful	*Morose*
Selfless	*Prideful*
Compassionate	*Ruthless*
Appealing to the Spirit	*Appealing to the Flesh*
Feel Right in the Gut	*Feel Wrong in the Gut*

with a tidy structure. Most of the time they are discombobulated babblings trying to work on problems in the future or the past.

In fact, I'll bet your inner storyteller is narrating at this very moment, telling you about something in your life. Test it out. Take 20 seconds or so to listen to the story you are hearing right now. Give it a chance; you'll be amazed at the stories being concocted and how divorced they are from the now.

I just took my own advice. I took three belly breaths and I started paying attention to the inner dialogue happening right now. Some voice sounding an awful lot like mine said, "Who are you to be writing a book? You're a mess!"

That story is independent of my actual experience. For goodness sakes, I'm having this accusatory thought while my fingers are on the keyboard and I am working on my goal. My fingers typing on the keyboard is my present moment reality. While taking action, I am in the now. As long as I am leaning into this moment, the nonsense fades.

The mind produces thoughts. That's just what it does—to the tune of 6,000 thoughts per day.[18] In order to discern whether these rapid-fire, repetitive stories are true, there must be some sort of standard. What is your standard of truth? How do you discern truth from deception?

Here is the key: In the midst of the monkey mind, you have a choice about who will be the arbiter of the conflicting messages. Relying on your raw feelings to tell you the truth while in an emotional crisis is not the best strategy.

While narrating the occasional positive story, the fickle mind will soon revert to tales of doom and gloom. Don't trust all the inner dialogue. Instead, put the stories you hear to the test through the lens of how God sees you. Decide what kind of Higher Power will be with you during the most mighty of storms. Go for it. Does the thought of God feel heavy and burdensome to you? Describe a supportive, loving, awesome presence that the mind can barely imagine. Now, pledge to yourself that your new personal concept of God will be the standard by which you will judge competing thoughts.

Rest assured, there is a storyteller greater than your own inner narrations. You have to listen carefully though, because the storyteller's voice rarely shouts. In fact, this voice of calm and peace often arises out of intense focus, stillness, or praise. This storyteller has already authored the greatest story of transformative love, and your own story is part of it.

Should you choose to follow these three practices, you will surely uncover stories about yourself that you didn't know existed. You'll realize just how prevalent the familiar stories are too. The more you place simple awareness on your story patterns, the more your stories come into alignment with your Higher Power's good and perfect will for your life.

Most forms of photography contain a message the photographer is trying to convey. In contrast, mindful photography allows you to simply be with a scene without layering in a bunch of commentary. Keep asking: "Will I judge this story in front of me, or just represent it?"

The mind is a lens through which you can observe and interpret the world. For this day, are you going to choose a clean, distortion-free lens showing God at the center of the scene? Or, will you go with that same old selfie lens that tells stories of a validation-seeking "me" as the hero in each shot?

In the end, mindfulness is not about our story at all. Yes, stories can be healthy. We spiritual beings naturally ponder dreams for our future. Without a doubt, a positive, powerful vision is an unstoppable force. But, the true inner peace you so desperately seek is the peace that comes from radical acceptance of the scene you are living out right now, through your senses and your soul.

After all, reality is the greatest story of all.

©2015 Lars Millberg

SHOW AND TELL

ALLOW ME TO *TELL* YOU A STORY

I remember when I was 5 and I had to do show and tell in front of my kindergarten class. I brought a personal item that my mom gave me and I felt embarrassed. I can't even remember what I brought but I vividly remember how I seized up with fear as I got up there to speak in front of everyone.

NOW, ALLOW ME TO *SHOW* YOU THE SAME STORY

Joe felt his tiny hand tremble as he pulled open the door to kindergarten class, day two. In his other hand he felt the dry and scratchy handles of the small canvas bag he carried. Today was show-and-tell day, and inside the bag was something special that his mom made for him. His knees felt like jelly as he walked across the classroom to his desk. He slid his little body into the cold wooden seat and placed his bag in his lap. His mouth felt dry and his hands were clammy. He gripped the bag handles so hard that his knuckles turned white. "I should have brought the toy dinosaur instead," he thought. "Everyone's gonna laugh at me." Just then, the teacher announced that it was Joe's turn to show and tell.

How do each of these stories land on you? Which one engages you most? How does your mind react to being *told* a story versus being *shown* the story, thus allowing you to interpret it through your own experience?

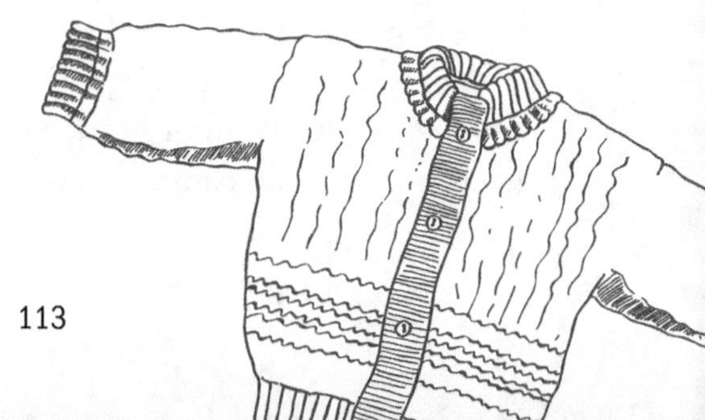

IS YOUR MIND SHOWING OR TELLING THE STORY OF THE SCENE IN FRONT OF YOU?

Stories lend an emotional charge to what we experience solely through our senses. Common sense tells us that these emotional projections on our surroundings often cloud our perception, and when they are habitual, they can cause great harm.

When you are out in the wild and you start to become dysregulated, you always have a chance to pause. During those moments, this practice can help you distinguish if you are "over-telling" a story. Do you ever feel like there is a narrator inside your mind, insisting on telling you distortions about yourself or your situation? If so, congratulate yourself on your self-awareness. Fortunately, the narrations are simply thoughts, and you are not your thoughts. Moreover, some thoughts are more aligned with your divine destiny than others. This is the moment of decision when you can turn away from darkness and towards the light. It's time to reach for the camera.

Through mindfulness, when you shift from telling to showing a painful story, you switch perspective and lessen the story's hold on yourself. The same can be true for a positive story that has turned into an attachment. I do it all the time. I find myself getting passionate about stories around "buying some mountain land" or "upgrading my career" or "being in a fantastic relationship."

It may very well be that these visions are signals of divine hope straight from God on High. But, leave it to me and I'll turn innocent dreams into demands of God. So, when I start repetitively dreaming my dreams and I feel those powerful body feelings from yearning for something I do not currently possess, I know that's a signal to get back to my senses. One more time, I gently place my hand on my heart mind take three deep belly breaths.

We are experiential beings. Take a risk for the next 10 seconds and try it now. Hand on heart, three belly breaths. Watch how it snaps you back into conscious awareness.

PLAY

Play with your stories through photography. Mess with assumptions. Shoot an ominous photo of a teddy bear, and then a hilarious photo of a tombstone. Distort something sacred. Capture something insignificant as if it were magnificent, like a selfie of you wearing a cape, heroically scrubbing a dirty toilet (if you actually own a cape you probably don't need much prodding). Shoot an image of your greatest dream as if it were something that could hold you back. That dream home of yours? Find an image of an unaffordable, high-interest mortgage on a property that won't sell. ·

Mindfully making "bad things seem good" and making "good things seem bad" isn't meant to be a buzz-kill for your dreams. On the contrary, this is an innocent, child-like opportunity to play and detach from the things that are holding you back. The more you can make your stories pliable, the less they distort your reality. The more you can laugh at your own identifications, the better. Identifications arise from the ego, and the ego is mighty crafty. Don't try to outsmart your ego. Instead, take it by the hand, get out into the world, and play around with it. Make peace with your crazy side through laughter. In this mad world, you can find plenty of inspiration for your inner comedian.

POV, STREET PORTRAITS, AND SHOW AND TELL

During several years living in Austin, I got deeply into street photography and vlogging, and eventually found a niche I call "street portraits." The YouTube videos I created from these street portrait encounters got tons of views, probably because they unintentionally nailed the balance between showing and telling.

Here was the formula: I went into the freak show of Austin's downtown streets with a GoPro attached to the top of my full-frame camera. The video from the GoPro provided a super-wide perspective while I walked around. On my camera I shot stills, usually through an 85mm lens, which functioned to isolate the subject.

Armed with my gear, I roamed the streets, GoPro rolling, showing these scenes as they unfolded. My point of view was your point of view. No commentary was needed. The super-wide GoPro POV was so stable and immersive that it was like you were in the scene right there with me, waiting to experience what happens next.

Invariably, I came across someone with an interesting face and energy. I gave them my little pitch and then worked with them to shoot several quick street portrait shots with the 85mm setup. Viewers of these vlogs saw what it was like, and they experienced all the awkward but heart-warming things as they happened spontaneously in the now.

The POV video perspective I am describing so far is the epitome of "showing" the street portrait experience. You are there with me, having your own experience, drawing your own conclusions versus me telling you what to think. But, the "showing" is only half of the formula of these vlogs.

Threaded throughout these videos is b-roll of the actual portrait shots that pop up for a few seconds as the shutter snaps. With these perfectly focused, shallow depth-of-field, meticulously edited street portraits, I was telling a story about the person in front of the lens. I knew that if I captured a person's portrait with a confident pose, using flattering lighting, while highlighting the subject's sincere, sparkling eyes, I was likely to evoke feel-good emotions from viewers. Of course, I could do the opposite too, framing my portrait subject in such a way that evoked a different feeling and projected a very different narrative. This is photographic storytelling.

With the combination of my GoPro story-showing videos and the juxtaposition of the story-telling stills, I created engaging videos that transported viewers into an immersive reality—almost a simulcast of the now.

SCENARIO:

You're taking a rare day off to enjoy nature. Despite how you should be feeling while walking up a beautiful shoreline, you're miserable. You miss the person you last took this stroll with, and the heartache is spiraling into a self-blame attack. The tears well up. You recognize it's time to intervene.

1. FOCUS on body and surroundings

- **HAND ON HEART** • **3 BELLY BREATHS** • **NOTE YOUR LEVEL OF PEACE**
- **OPEN YOUR EYES**

With your eyes closed or gazing softly, gently place your hand on your heart and take three deep belly breaths. Simply feel your various body sensations. Note your level of inner peace. Open your eyes wide and take in what is surrounding you. Just "be" for a few seconds without commentary or categorizations.

2. CAPTURE the present moment

- **ACT OPPOSITE TO EMOTION** • **TURN SMARTPHONE INTO CAMERA**
- **PHOTOGRAPH MINDFULLY** • **NOTE YOUR LEVEL OF PEACE**

Note your resistance to this practice and choose action anyway. Demonstrate your aim to experience inner peace by turning your smartphone into a camera, with airplane mode on. Now, wipe off your lenses and get your body to the best place to capture a few mindful shots.

While walking up that beautiful beach shoreline—the one with the painful memories—you are making the choice to create new memories there. You are setting out to take the story out of the scene, and to simply focus on presenting the sand, the sea, and the sky. Catch some macro-sparkles in the sand down low. Snap the shutter as the foam laps your lens. Shoot the giant sky with the sea as just a sliver at the bottom of the frame. Shoot down at your own two feet glistening in the sand, stable and sufficient, just like you. Now you are layering powerful new energy into that scene. You are accepting what was once there, and capturing what is there now.

Remain present while editing, capturing the look of the moment. Delete all but a few sacred photos. Pronounce your collection "complete" and do another hand-on-heart check-in of your inner peace.

3. SHINE your light on someone

• LOVE SOMEONE • STAY OFF SOCIAL MEDIA • NOTE YOUR LEVEL OF PEACE

Ready to transcend the enticing familiarity of self-pity and fear? Shine your light and bless others through your mindful photos. You'll create loving connections and redirect your attention to the eternal. Refrain from sharing your creations on social media. Instead, bless someone directly with your photos. Notice how you get lost in the moment when you connect with someone's heart. Hand on your heart, do one last check-in of your inner peace.

Congratulations on creating a new memory. Your final images deserve a home. Drop them into a folder on your phone called "new memories." Own the courage it takes to do that. Notice how it feels to act with intention about the road ahead. Each time you flex your mindful muscles like this, not allowing the past to dictate your future, you gain strength to do it again and again, recreating your life.

JOURNAL PROMPTS

∞ *As you open your eyes to the scene around you, can you spot an object that has a negative emotional charge? What is the story behind that object?*

∞ *Describe the experience of feeling your uncomfortable body sensations but photographing the dark-feeling object anyway. Were you able to capture the object in a beautiful or funny way? I'll let you in on a little secret. My eyes landed on a bottle of medication that I hate to take. I couldn't quite pull off a beautiful photo of the bottle, so I resorted to a funny shot instead. I'll leave the medication and the crude thing I just did with it to your imagination.*

∞ *By layering new visual memories upon old and not allowing the past to dictate your future, did you notice a positive shift in power? Describe it. Instead of a shift towards positive energy, did this practice make you feel like getting in bed with the covers pulled up to your chin? Describe that. Back to my silly example, now that I've had a belly laugh, the energy of that little yellow pill jar has shifted. It no longer has power over me.*

FORKING STORIES

"My double vision always seems to get the best of me,
the best of me, yeah
Ooh, double vision, I need my double vision
It takes me out of my head,
takin' me out of my head"

"DOUBLE VISION" SONG BY FOREIGNER

This practice is designed to help you experience inner peace through the mindful photography technique of "forking," where you get to identify and deliberately choose which mental pathways align with your truth, and which ones split off into a storyline at odds with your true nature.

Have you ever been to one of those audience-participation plays, where the audience gets to choose the ending? I read about a playwright in San Francisco named Daniel Heath who created a work called *Forking!*, in which the audience gets 20-plus chances to vote on which fork the story should take. The play changes from night to night, varying from dark and gloomy to light-hearted and hilarious. Each fork in the road is up to the audience.

Just like the play, your mind presents you with choice after choice. Since you are independent of your thoughts, you have freedom to choose which energetic pathways to proceed down. Each time you make the courageous choice and interrupt old patterns of thought, you become more emotionally resilient. Uncontested, competing truths bouncing around in your head can hold you back, trapping you in an endless loop of second-guessing.

Hopefully by now you have already made an intentional list of the characteristics of your personal Higher Power. Those are the qualities by which you will judge your stories' truthfulness. Commit to mindfully sit with stories as they come up, breathing into them. As you create a little space, you allow your inner spirit to choose which stories are liberating and helpful for your ongoing spiritual growth, and which stories are limiting your access to the blessings of grace.

I can personally attest that mindful photography practices that heighten awareness of our looping stories can be liberating. Like that wacky interactive play in San Francisco, you get to choose the next branch in your plot, and the next, and the next. Come good or bad, you can always take the next right action. You'll get better and better at quickly noticing dark pathways and turning towards choices that are energetically best for you and your growth. Expect clarity and freedom from this practice. What the fork do you have to lose?

SCENARIO:

Your supervisor just brought a mistake to your attention. By the time you are back at your desk, your mind is racing.

1. FOCUS on body and surroundings

• HAND ON HEART • 3 BELLY BREATHS • NOTE YOUR LEVEL OF PEACE • OPEN YOUR EYES

With your eyes closed or gazing softly, gently place your hand on your heart and take three deep belly breaths. Simply feel your various body sensations. Note your level of inner peace. Open your eyes wide and take in what is surrounding you. Just "be" for a few seconds without commentary or categorizations.

2. CAPTURE the present moment

• ACT OPPOSITE TO EMOTION • TURN SMARTPHONE INTO CAMERA
• PHOTOGRAPH MINDFULLY • NOTE YOUR LEVEL OF PEACE

Note your resistance to this practice and choose action anyway. Demonstrate your aim to experience inner peace by turning your smartphone into a camera, with airplane mode on. Now, wipe off your lenses, get up, and head outside for a walk around the block. What your boss told you really rocked your confidence and triggered an old familiar story pattern. Growing up, you learned to associate making mistakes with harsh consequences. You are hardly out the door and the narration begins. "How in the hell could I have made that mistake again? No matter how hard I try I always make some error that ruins the whole thing. Good luck applying for the supervisor position. Clearly I don't have my act together for that yet."

When I intervene on stories that distort my career or financial situation, I like to quickly explore the first act of the play where I lose everything and wind up living under a railway bridge or under a thorny bush. What is your go-to drama story that emerges when your security feels threatened? Does that align with your belief in a God who always cares for your physical needs?

Take courage and play with your prickly story of living under a bush. "Aha! That bush over there is actually kind of pretty and I bet the rent is next to nothing. I think I'll go over there and take some shots of how a mattress might fit underneath."

Minutes later, you sneak back to your desk, chuckling under your breath. You're back to presence.

Remain present while editing, capturing the look of the moment. Delete all but a few sacred photos. Pronounce your collection "complete" and do another hand-on-heart check-in of your inner peace.

3. SHINE your light on someone

• LOVE SOMEONE • STAY OFF SOCIAL MEDIA • NOTE YOUR LEVEL OF PEACE

The shots you took of the bush around the block from the office are epic. Of the bunch, you kept three and edited them to show the features of your new low-cost bright-green home in a thorny bush. About that time you remember a conversation you had yesterday with your buddy Johnny who has some similar hangups. You send him the photo with the following note: "Hey dude! Today at work the boss corrected a typo of mine and the next thing I knew I was living under this bush. Come join me in cray-cray land. Plenty of room for you!"

Now, you giggle at Johnny's hilarious reply, and you do one last hand-on-heart check-in of your inner peace.

Mission accomplished. Welcome to the now.

JOURNAL PROMPTS

∞ *What real-world scenario came up that forced you to choose what the fork direction you were going to take?*

∞ *"Each time you make the courageous choice and interrupt old patterns of thought, you become more emotionally resilient." What body sensations come up as you ponder this idea?*

∞ *Were you able to get a laugh out of someone with your mindful photo? Do you associate laughter with mindfulness? Why or why not?*

A mentor who was influential in my life used to gently bring me back to the question: "What are the possibilities?" No matter how stuck I felt, that question would always loosen me up long enough to realize that I always have the freedom of choice and the power to take action. Baseball legend Yogi Berra couldn't have summed it up better: "When you come to a fork in the road, take it."

PHOTO TIP: SHOOT WITH A BLACK AND WHITE FILTER

Everyone knows you can convert color photos to black and white after the fact. But did you know you can actually *shoot* in black and white? Locate the black and white filter on your camera app, and then everything you see on screen will be previewed in shades of gray. Removing color from a scene forces us to look for shapes of dark and light, versus the strong colors begging for our attention. Try it on your next outing, and note your level of presence.

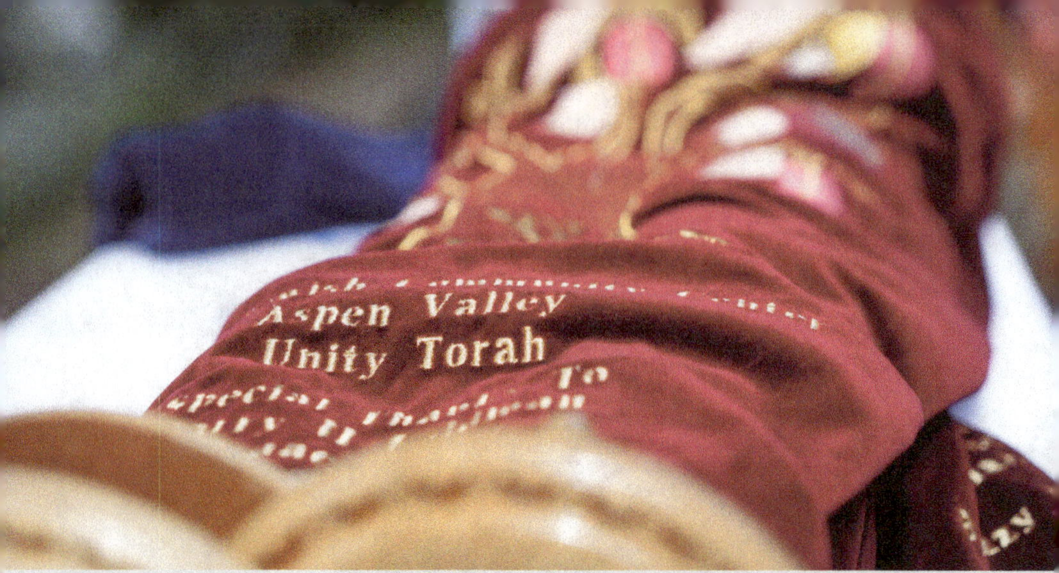

Aspen Valley
Unity Torah

WORK THE SCENE

"What you think upon grows. Whatever you allow to occupy your mind you magnify in your life. Whether the subject of your thought be good or bad, the law works and the condition grows. Any subject that you keep out of your mind tends to diminish in your life, because what you do not use atrophies. The more you think of grievances, the more such trials you will continue to receive; the more you think of the good fortune you have had, the more good fortune will come to you."

Emmet Fox

This practice is designed to help you experience inner peace through the mindful photography technique of "working the scene." Just as a photojournalist uses every angle necessary to tell a story, we will describe our present reality from multiple perspectives. You will increase your mental flexibility and capacity to imagine divinely-inspired possibilities. Most of all, you'll have fun capturing images representing a broader view of your reality.

Let's face it, hyper-focusing on unsolved problems produces disempowering fear. Have you ever noticed that the very act of intensively trying to solve a problem often makes the problem larger? I believe that the law of attraction is built into the universe, and one of the law's basic tenets is "what we think upon grows."

When you become hijacked by mental projections towards the past or future, you get tunnel vision. It's like your mind is a camera

(left) A bat mitzvah that I shot professionally, with a full-frame camera. Event photographers "work the scene," making sure to capture detail shots, wide shots, and everything in-between.

8 WAYS TO WORK THE SCENE

1. SHOOT HORIZONTALLY

Be a photographer. Take your work seriously. Stop shooting photos vertically. You can always re-purpose and chop a vertical photo out of a horizontal, but you can't make a horizontal out of a vertical. Just because the button is at the bottom of the screen doesn't mean you should shoot photos vertically. God put your eyes side by side for a reason.

2. SHOOT WIDE

Switch to your widest lens and shoot the scene in front of you. Focus on layers. For example: close-up of a sandy foot hanging off an Adirondack chair, soft-focused kids playing on the beach, blurry sailboat in background. That's a layered scene. Try using this technique to tell a story in one photo.

3. SHOOT TIGHT OR TINY

Back to our beach scene, imagine a ground-level shot of a shore break splashing against your lens, an up-close abstract of part of a sandcastle, and a macro shot of a teeny crab or piece of seaweed.

4. USE LEADING LINES

Look for natural or man-made lines that can lead the viewer's eye into your photo. Shoot super-wide, get low, and aim down the beach, with shore on one half of the frame and sea on the other half, so that the water meets the shore midframe. Marvel at how all the lines converge at the center of the frame down the beach towards a converging point in the horizon.

5. WTF?

Find something to shoot in such a way that makes it nearly impossible to discern. Perhaps a cropped shot of the curve of a shiny red plastic sand pail, blue sky in background. Is that the side of a building? Is it big or is it small? Send it to someone who could use a laugh.

6. FIND PATTERNS

Shoot a macro shot of a shell, trim the edges off, and highlight a pattern instead of the object itself. Take some close-ups of bright watermelon with a pattern of black seeds.

7. COMPOSE

Turn grid lines on for your camera. Experiment with rules of thirds. Break the rules. Make the sky the top 90% and the earth a sliver in the lower 10%. Combine multiple ways to work the scene and notice the effect it has on you. Do some abstracts with odd compositions. Take a shot with the horizon off just a bit and send it to a photo-snob without explanation. Notice how funny we perfectionists are as your ego convulses. These are all amusing ways to engage with the now.

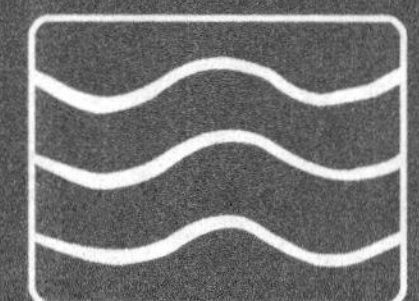

8. SHOOT WEIRD

A piece of driftwood comes to your attention. A big hole in it makes the perfect frame as you shoot through it, focused on the seascape behind.

with a macro lens that can only focus on one tiny thing at a time. Swapping out your mental macro lens for a super-wide angle lens will enable a "big picture" mindset, promoting acceptance and insight.

FIRST, LET'S EXPLORE THIS IDEA OF "WORKING THE SCENE" PHOTOGRAPHICALLY

In event photography, you learn to get a variety of shots that serve to tell the complete story of the occasion. Imagine a new couple paging through their wedding album for the first time. What might be pleasing to them, helping preserve memories of that special day?

In this imaginary album, you might see a wide shot, looking down the center aisle of the church. On the next page you may see tighter shots of the couple during the ceremony. Then come the detail shots, like their rings and other sacred items. You might even see a cute shot of that moment when the 4 year-old ring bearer had a mini-meltdown before finally walking down the aisle. Wedding reception shots might include the cake topper, buffet line, parents posing, couples dancing, and jubilant audience reactions to the garter toss.

Get the picture? The album is perfect because it tells the complete story of the event.

But, imagine the look on the couple's faces if they opened their album and it only had one photo inside—that of the 4-year-old's red face and crocodile tears? Out of context, that's a sad and incomplete part of a larger, joyful story.

If your world seems dark and limited right now, take courage. Boldly invite in all the body sensations that accompany life's hassles. Breathe into them. Show them who's boss by stepping out in faith, knowing that these mindful photography practices will transport you to another plane of awareness.

Let's focus on having fun and improving our photography skills while we're at it.

SCENARIO:

These photographic techniques can lighten your load in a variety of scenarios. They work by absorbing you in and showing objects and situations from all perspectives—macro through telephoto.

1. FOCUS on body and surroundings

• HAND ON HEART • 3 BELLY BREATHS • NOTE YOUR LEVEL OF PEACE
• OPEN YOUR EYES

With your eyes closed or gazing softly, gently place your hand on your heart and take three deep belly breaths. Simply feel your various body sensations. Note your level of inner peace. Open your eyes wide and take in what is surrounding you. Just "be" for a few seconds without commentary or categorizations.

2. CAPTURE the present moment

• ACT OPPOSITE TO EMOTION • TURN SMARTPHONE INTO CAMERA
• PHOTOGRAPH MINDFULLY • NOTE YOUR LEVEL OF PEACE

Note your resistance to this practice and choose action anyway. Demonstrate your aim to experience inner peace by turning your smartphone into a camera, with airplane mode on. Now, wipe off your lenses and get your body to the best place to capture a few mindful shots. Remain present while editing, capturing the look of the moment. Delete all but a few sacred photos. Pronounce your collection "complete" and do another hand-on-heart check-in of your inner peace.

3. SHINE your light on someone

• LOVE SOMEONE • STAY OFF SOCIAL MEDIA • NOTE YOUR LEVEL OF PEACE

Ready to transcend the enticing familiarity of self-pity and fear? Shine your light and bless others through your mindful photos. You'll create loving connections and redirect your attention to the eternal. Refrain from sharing your creations on social media. Instead, bless someone directly with your photos. Notice how you get lost in the moment when you connect with someone's heart. Hand on your heart, do one last check-in of your inner peace.

You know the adage, "if you want to really learn something, teach it?" For this practice, why not send a friend one of your creations, explaining the technique you are using. Describe how you felt while shooting and editing your image. Challenge them to shoot with the same technique and send it back to you. Notice how it feels to experience photo-sharing in a new way, engaging with someone positively.

JOURNAL PROMPTS

∞ *What is your reaction when you receive mental reminders to breathe into your body and take note of your level of peace?*

∞ *"Work the Scene" can apply to endless scenarios, from little Maria's 5th birthday party to your company's annual event. What kind of scene did you get to "work?" Which ways to work the scene did you get to practice? How did they work for you?*

∞ *American theoretical physicist Richard Feynman said: "If you want to master something, teach it." Has that been true for you? What happens to your level of presence while you are showing someone a new technique?*

Examples of working a scene, beach vacation-style. I was invited along on this one week extended-family getaway at a Florida beachfront property. At the time I wasn't able to match the financial generosity of others who made the trip possible, but I could contribute my God-given gift of photography. After everyone received these, I felt so much love reading their kind words of thanks. Freezing moments in time like this is a downright miracle. Spreading this joy can last lifetimes.

These particular shots, taken with a full-frame camera, are of a simple trip down to the beach. I caught action shots of boogie-boarders, shown in the context of family cheering them on. There is a shot of the house, and the huge expanse of water and sky that the house overlooks. While shooting a scene, it is a mindful experience to include artistic shots, like this low and tight photo of foam rolling over sand, leading the eye to the converging horizon. And finally, I was able to capture some couple-portrait shots of cherished moments.

SURRENDER CONTROL LET GO OF THE PAST

*"God, grant me the serenity
to accept the things I cannot change,
courage to change the things I can,
and the wisdom to know the difference."*

THE SERENITY PRAYER

If you find yourself trapped in a state of lack, these practices will help you find lasting freedom. Gratitude is a portal to inner peace. Practicing gratitude is a reliable way to enter a mindful state in the here and now. This tool is available to you at all waking moments. A grateful state is a mindful state. These mindful photography exercises will immediately elevate you to a higher plane. And the great thing is, you don't have to "get" anything to reach it.

The following practices will help you loosen your grip a bit. When I started delving into practices like these, I noticed some things that were holding me back. I thought I had the past mostly mopped up, but I didn't. Fear was clinging on to past hurts. For some reason, I felt less wrong when I focused on how I was wronged. Oh, the insanity of the mind.

(left) Ever walk around your hustling, bustling town with your mind making as much noise as a subway train? And if that weren't enough, each corner you turn has another old, tired memory. You can use mindful photography to lay claim to the place where your feet stand.

So, let's practice giving up control and letting go of the past. What do you have to lose? After all, constantly feeling like a victim of outside circumstances is miserable.

In this section you'll use some creative, engaging mindful photography practices to train yourself to keep turning towards God and relinquishing your feeble attempts to control people, places, and things outside of yourself. Remember, all you can do is the inner work of turning from defeating thoughts to presence, repeatedly. Each time you do a practice, you are practicing letting go.

Letting go is a bear I struggle like hell with. At the time of writing this, I'm four years after a divorce and all the hurts, resentments, and regrets are still painful when I allow my attention to dwell on them. I cannot control the arising of thoughts, but I can control the action I take in response. I remember not-too-many years ago feeling so powerless to respond to these powerful emotional attachments. I would simply crater in the face of self-defeating thought patterns. Trust me my friend, I know it's not easy. But I also know from years of practice that each time you turn your attention away from the magnet of self-pity and towards a mindful practice instead, you strengthen your muscles of resilience.

As the saying goes, we get to decide at this moment, this day, how we are going to contribute to the dash on our respective tombstones. Therefore, there is no sense beating yourself up for the past.

We are all spiritual works in progress. Accept the fact that in the past you may have lost a great deal of peaceful presence while consumed with unproductive worry. You can't go back and change that. But right here, right now, you can practice just being. Eternity is in this moment. Quick! Take a picture of it.

Ready to get fearlessly mindful? Fellow students, this section is grad-school level. With compassion and patience, you are going to face some demons that have kept you in fear. Through practice, you won't shy away from difficult body sensations that arise from photographing things you don't want to face, or tidying up old photos of memories you'd rather not experience. Yes, it's hard, but you can do hard things. Resisting fear and acting opposite to emotion is powerful, transformative mindfulness. As you read this, picture yourself succeeding at these practices and feeling immediate results. In these moments of presence you will find freedom from powerful identifications that produce the mental noise that keeps you from present moment peace. I pray that through deeply letting go, all your mourning will turn into dancing.

I love the spaciousness of scenes like these. My mind feels less cluttered when I practice forgiveness and letting go. Shot near Rifle, Colorado.

SACRED PRUNING

*"The best way to find out what we really need
is to get rid of what we don't."*

Marie Kondo

Sacred pruning is the mindful photography practice of getting rid of undesirable or excess photos, removing the superfluous. You are going to experience the mindful peace that comes with clearing out the old and making space for the new. Technology has allowed us to amass personal photo collections on the scale of the Library of Congress. If all those photos were in banker's boxes in your home, you might have to build tunnels to move around. Look through your collection of ten-thousand selfies and compare that to the small stack of worn, yellowed prints from your childhood. What's the difference? Those old prints are rare and sacred.

Years ago, there was a reality show called *Tidying Up with Marie Kondo*, featuring the petite, soft-spoken Japanese woman who went into pack-rats' homes and brought sanity to out-of-control clutter. I was drawn to this series because I always noticed how unsettled I felt while I am around clutter, whether that be in my home, my computer's desktop, or my (gulp!) photo folder on my phone.

What I loved about Marie Kondo's methodology is that she would go into a bedroom, for example, and pile every bit of a clos-

(left) Lord have mercy! Your faithful author needs to practice what he preaches. Here is a screen shot of my photo library from years back. Zoomed way out it looks pretty cool. However, when I zoom in, these photos turn into a bunch of happy memories interspersed with a haunted house of past ghosts. Ready to join me for some sacred pruning?

et's contents ceiling-high on top of the bed. Then she asked participants to go through each item, one at a time. The person held up each item, felt the item's energy, and kept only those things that sparked joy in them. When an object had a heavy energy or was simply no longer needed, people were taught to bless the item and then pitch it for good. The psychological effects on the participants were astounding, and research on clutter backs up this phenomenon.

Researchers have conducted studies on how people perform and feel in tidy versus messy environments. Research suggests that "clean organized environments" benefit people psychologically, from clearer thought processes to increased confidence and abilities.[19]

Predictably, research also shows that an untidy environment can negatively impact human health. Mood and stress levels, memory capabilities, and even the ability to process other people's facial expressions are impacted negatively. When people's personal space is "de-cluttered," they are better able to sleep, focus, and hold feelings of life-satisfaction.

IDEAS FOR SACREDLY PRUNING YOUR PHOTOS AND YOUR MIND

1. USE NEW WINESKINS

Jesus used a story about putting new wine into old, leather wineskins to teach about the pliability of our hearts and minds. New wine would cause used wineskins to burst. To grow, your mind must become like fresh wineskins, where you humbly allow a shift in consciousness to fill you from this point forward. So, as you embark on the ongoing process of "tidying up" your photos, take it easy on yourself. Draw a line and change your habits from here forward, versus trying to clean up a giant library sequentially. You'll eventually create a system that fits you and gives you the benefits of decluttering your photos. The point isn't so much to accomplish your photo reorganization, but rather to be present during the process and allow only the best images to remain so you nourish your soul and that of others.

2. CLEAR THE BEAVER DAMS

Beavers can be pesky neighbors to humans. Their fortified dams are sometimes cleared because they can back up water, killing trees and wreaking havoc in developed areas. In nature, streams can get cut off for many reasons, creating stagnant ponds that were once part of fresh flowing, crystal-clear water.

Metaphorically speaking, if your photo library is jammed full of old, rotten junk, your creative flow will be restricted. Need proof? Reach for your phone and scroll through the last few months' worth of photos. Switch to "yearly" view and behold your library of 10,000 images, 80% of which you'd never miss if they were miraculously zapped away. Feel the heaviness in your body when you try to wrap your head around this unculled mess. Close your eyes and envision a revamped photo library that you'd be happy to leave behind to your loved ones. Be present with that feeling.

3. FOLDERS ARE YOUR FRIEND

During this process, create a simple system of folders where you can mindfully tuck away your sacred memories. For instance, imagine you have a few minutes to spare and you start thumbing through some old photos on your phone. You come across your daughter Maria's 5th birthday party photos from a few years back—all 57 of them. Minutes later, you've fearlessly blessed and deleted all but a half-dozen or so. Tuck your hero shots into a folder named "Maria-5th birthday." Imagine you showing these at her wedding in 20 years. Now, do a little body check and notice how this brief practice brought you satisfaction.

4. HAVE A GOD BOX

Suppose you are smiling away, being present while organizing delightful photo memories, and deleting less-interesting shots. In an instant, your mood shifts. That darned shot is staring at you yet again. It may be a photo of your father during a challenging time in your relationship. It might be of someone lost to you now, reminding you of how much healing you still need. Or, it may be a dream that you gave up on, but revisiting it now is just too painful.

When you come across images like this, take a quick minute of action. Simply export them to a folder on your drive and delete them from your photo library. Name the folder "God Box." They are in a sacred place now, always accessible if you choose to "go there," but where they are not is in your face, disturbing you over and over again for years each time you scroll past them.

Can you feel the lightness that comes from intentionally dealing with something that robs you of peace? And who knows? Perhaps years from now you'll peek into your God Box and you'll realize many photos inside now represent something different, or have lost their negative charge entirely.

5. KILL SOME DREAMS

"Killing dreams" sounds downright sacrilegious, doesn't it? "You're telling me to kill dreams? My dreams are all I'm hanging on to. Sometimes they feel like the only things keeping me alive!"

As you peruse your photos, take inventory of your past dreams. You may come across a scanned image of an old print showing you in a firefighter outfit. You're not a firefighter now, but you do love your current career. Are you a failure because you aren't a firefighter? Of course not. That childhood dream is no longer relevant in your life.

Many "dreams" may in fact be holding you back, making you feel like a failure. Imagine being a child brought up in a well-to-do family. Dad's vision of success involved lots of expensive hobbies, each with its own set of toys. You took a different path. You serve and bless people by being a teacher, or a police officer, or an artist. You truly found your calling. How sad would it be if, despite your successes in your field, you continually compared yourself to your childhood benchmark for success: material wealth.

It's time to let those old dreams die a dignified death. They served a purpose once, but now they rob you of your peace. Back to your photo library, you come across that iconic family photo of you and your family in front of your parents' vacation home. How many times have you looked at that photo enviously? Pause. Zoom in on that image. Bless each person in that photo. Zoom back out to the entire scene as you thank your Higher Power for your life and the unique path you have been allowed to walk in this life.

SCENARIO:

You just fired off your phone's photo app, searching for certain photos you want to show at a going away party for a coworker. Scrolling and scrolling, you notice your breath is shallow and your body is tense. You take a deep, mindful breath and two things dawn on you. First, your library looks like an episode out of a hoarder reality show. And second, you notice that there are certain photos that provoke bad feelings each time you see them. You want to avoid that bad energy, yet the photos remain, year after year.

1. FOCUS on body and surroundings

- HAND ON HEART • 3 BELLY BREATHS • NOTE YOUR LEVEL OF PEACE
- OPEN YOUR EYES

As this practice often happens spontaneously while you are reviewing your photos, remember to do a body check-in by gently placing your hand on your heart and taking three deep belly breaths. Simply feel your various body sensations and note your level of inner peace. Just "be" for a few seconds with your images without commentary or categorizations.

2. CAPTURE the present moment

- ACT OPPOSITE TO EMOTION • TURN SMARTPHONE INTO CAMERA
- PHOTOGRAPH MINDFULLY • NOTE YOUR LEVEL OF PEACE

Note your resistance to this practice and choose action anyway. Demonstrate your aim to experience inner peace by turning your smartphone into a camera, with airplane mode on. Take on one batch of photos at a time, deleting all but a sacred few. Create a folder with your favorites from the event, pronounce your collection "complete," and do another hand-on-heart check-in of your inner peace.

3. SHINE your light on someone

• LOVE SOMEONE • STAY OFF SOCIAL MEDIA • NOTE YOUR LEVEL OF PEACE

Ready to transcend the enticing familiarity of self-pity and fear? Shine your light and bless others through your mindful photos. You'll create loving connections and redirect your attention to the eternal. Refrain from sharing your creations on social media. Instead, bless someone directly with your photos. Notice how you get lost in the moment when you connect with someone's heart.

In our scenario, you were searching for memorable photos of a special coworker. Not only are you feeling relieved from finding some great shots and organizing them, but you are also feeling that "ahh" satisfaction that comes from decluttering. Send that fresh folder of a sacred few images along with a kind note to your coworker and make their day. Hand on your heart, do one last check-in of your inner peace.

JOURNAL PROMPTS

∞ *When you ponder the closet in your home that is stacked to the ceiling with things you haven't needed in years, what body sensations come up? Remember, "anxiety" or "overwhelm" isn't a body sensation. Instead, use descriptors like "facial muscles constricting," "tingles and nausea in my belly," and "tightness in my chest."*

∞ *In our "Capture the Present Moment" instructions, we note our resistance to the Sacred Pruning practice and (hopefully) choose action anyway. What do you resist about throwing unneeded things away? After you take action and tidy up a sock drawer or set of images, take note of the sense of satisfaction you feel? Describe it. Do images seem more special when they are specially chosen and organized? How so?*

∞ *Technology allows us to search our photo library by face, creating folders for different people. Imagine doing that. Among the special memories, there might be a folder or two that contains past relationships you have processed and largely moved past. Yet, every time you come across them, you feel a heaviness. How would it feel to delete those photos permanently in an attempt to eradicate the tough memories? For some trauma-filled memories, this may be necessary. However, it may also be healthy to simply export those images to our previously-mentioned "God Box" folder on your local drive, and delete all of that person's images from your active photo library. What comes up as you make these tough decisions? What do you think the cumulative effect might eventually have on your inner peace?*

"A place for everything, everything in its place," said Ben Franklin. *Sacred, intentionally-chosen photos are worthy of proper folders and naming conventions. Orphaned socks, dead winter leaves, and camping-spot trash once served a purpose; now they can be put out of sight permanently. Out with the old, and in with the new. Do you have a little memento that is too painful to toss out? No biggie. Put it in your God Box and let it go for now. It'll be in good hands.*

PHOTO TIP: SCREEN SHOTS

A "screen shot" is simply a photo of your phone or computer screen. On an iPhone, click the side button and the volume up button at the same time. A screen shot can come in handy when you receive a compliment or note of encouragement. Put these treasures in a folder named "I'm friggin' awesome!" and take a peek in there from time to time to remind yourself how much you matter.

FORGIVENESS

"Forgiveness is fundamentally for our own sake, for our own mental health. It is a way to let go of the pain we carry. This is illustrated by the story of two ex-prisoners of war who meet after many years. When the first one asks, 'Have you forgiven your captors yet?' the second man answers, 'No, never.' 'Well then,' the first man replies, 'they still have you in prison.'"

JACK KORNFIELD

Forgiveness is the embodiment of surrendering control and letting go of the past. When your thoughts are consumed with hurtful memories, forgiveness is a dependable path to self-awareness and the now. In this practice you will use mindful photography techniques to liberate yourself from unforgiveness. In the process you will explore new meanings and applications of its liberating power.

Mindful photography is a great tool for forgiveness because it freezes a symbolic image in a moment in time and allows us to process forgiveness through our visual sense. Our visual sense is so powerful. We point our eyes at one thing and all sorts of emotional responses ensue. We redirect our eyes to another thing and still other body sensations follow.

(left) Aren't creative "mistakes" delightful? Seasons ago, I thought this user-error might be useful someday. Fast forward to this book, I couldn't have found a more fitting image of how unforgiveness can so easily hold me captive and distort my view. The good news about the prison of unforgiveness? We always hold the escape-key.

Right now, is there something you can glance at that reminds you of past pain or trauma? I just looked over at a throw pillow cover that triggered a wince of pain in my heart. Silly, isn't it? How can an object be so charged with emotion? And how can we possibly muster the strength to confront the actual source of the pain? My answer to that question is simple: you can't do it through your own strength. You have to tap into a greater current of strength. Through mindfulness, you can calm the mental noise enough to access that power.

Forgiveness may be the most profound and challenging of all spiritual practices. It takes humility and guts to forgive. It forces you to the cliff-edge of ego to confront your dark shadows.

Personally, I easily gravitate towards victimhood and self-pity. I cling to unforgiveness to protect myself from past wounds. One internal conversation I hear quite frequently is, "She was the one at fault, and I didn't deserve that." As usual, my ego denies involvement. It sucks to admit that in that relationship when there was a problem, I was commonly at the center of it. But once I do admit it, God has something to work with. It puts me in a humble state, admitting that no matter what another person did that hurt me, I am the one who needs healing and freedom.

FORGIVE THROUGH DIVINE POWER, NOT YOUR OWN POWER

Whoever genuinely hurt you might have affected the trajectory of your life. An adult might have saddened your childhood. No one is immune to past pain and trauma. Everyone has been abandoned, abused, hit, hurt, deceived, slandered, or cheated at some point in life. How then, under our own power, can we transcend that profound wounding? To achieve that, you have to dig deep spiritually and rely on an almighty inner power, combined with the power of mindfulness.

What object in your view reminded you of past pain or trauma? What was your "pillow?" Once you identify it, ask yourself, "Do I want to be free?" How would you like to decouple from that negative energy?

I made a promise at the beginning of this book that I would always practice what I preach, and I'd never tell you something was a good therapeutic technique that didn't actually work for me. So, here is what I did with my pillow.

This pillow has lived in a few places. It came from a little shop in Aspen, the kind of place you pop into with your spouse on a road trip together. Back in Texas, it sat on "our" couch, but it represented my dream of living in the mountains again.

My worn, discolored, much-flatter pillow now sits on my bed. Ironically, I live down the road from Aspen now. Since I moved here, Frankie the Doodle and I have been on adventures to several Colorado destinations stitched on that pillow. It has propped up my back while writing this book. It gets dirty because, well, there's a lot of dirt around here. The Doodle and I have drug in black dirt from alpine hikes, red dirt from river trips, and everything in between. I guess you could say the pillow has particles of dirt on it from a whole lot of gorgeous places and beautiful memories.

I put my smartphone on airplane mode, take a few deep breaths, and look at the photo of my touristy pillow case. I begin by thanking it for being my companion in recent years on this most amazing adventure of my life here in the Rockies. I go back a little farther in time and thank it for being something I'd smile at when I lived back in Texas, longing to go back to the mountains. As painful as it is, I summon courage, and in my memory I go back even farther to that day in the little shop in Aspen when we bought the pillow. Looking at my snapshot, I forgive that moment. I forgive her. I forgive the present moment of uncertainty. I forgive myself. I ask God's forgiveness. I take back any ties that bind me to past pain.

Through mindful photography I can be fully present with feelings surrounding unforgiveness. I can take action to confront my fears and dismantle my ego, if even for a moment. I turn to my pillow photo one last time and ask with a grin, "What other adventures await us?" Now the energy associated with my Colorado pillow feels totally different. This is where my path has taken me, and I am free.

SCENARIO:

In the previous practice, you learned about objects and how they trigger emotions. You've experienced the lightness that comes from purging your surroundings of lots of things you no longer want or need. However, you may still have objects around you that seem to be charged with heavy energy. This morning, like clockwork, that dreadful energy arises again. On your way out the door of you and your spouse's rickety old house, the inside door knob comes off in your hand. "Doh! I just tried to fix this!" You slam the door shut, twist the key to lock up, and head out to your car fuming. As you throw the car into reverse, self-condemnation floods in. "If I made more money I wouldn't have to live in this dump! Why didn't I get that raise? I'm terrible at fixing things and I have been since I was a kid."

1. FOCUS on body and surroundings

• HAND ON HEART • 3 BELLY BREATHS • NOTE YOUR LEVEL OF PEACE
• OPEN YOUR EYES

Before you reach the end of the driveway, you feel tension throughout your body and notice you are hardly breathing. You return the gear shifter to park. You close your eyes and gently place your hand on your heart while you take three deep belly breaths. You simply feel your various body sensations, and note your level of inner peace.

Your eyes open wide and you take in what is surrounding you. Just "being" for a few seconds without commentary or categorizations is already helping to calm you down.

2. CAPTURE the present moment

• ACT OPPOSITE TO EMOTION • TURN SMARTPHONE INTO CAMERA • PHOTOGRAPH MINDFULLY • NOTE YOUR LEVEL OF PEACE

As you gaze through the windshield, you notice an architectural detail of your old wooden house. "They sure don't build 'em like that anymore," you think. A thought occurs to you: "Take the shot." Resistance shows up. "I'll be late if I do." You made a commitment to your emotional health, so you choose action anyway. Within seconds you are standing at the curb, taking a wide shot of your old house. You trot up to the front porch, unlock the creaky front door, and duck inside for an-

other quick shot. The worn and wobbly glass door knob still hangs on to the door. You smile as you take a tight shot of it, light sparkling inside.

As you slide back into your car, you do a quick hand-on-heart check-in of your inner peace. You drive off a little more peacefully.

3. SHINE your light on someone

• LOVE SOMEONE • STAY OFF SOCIAL MEDIA • NOTE YOUR LEVEL OF PEACE

Now at work, you pull up those two shots of your home from an hour earlier. This morning, you are going to shine your light and practice self-forgiveness. Gazing at your quick shots, a memory returns. The wide photo of your home resembles the original photo you saw of your home's listing many years ago. Tears well up as you remember you and your newlywed spouse hugging each other when you learned that the bank approved your mortgage, right around this time of the year—the holiday season. What memories you have shared since then.

Somehow your energy shifts from focusing on your shortcomings to focusing on your blessings. You surrender control over peeling paint, a creaking porch, and the fact that you aren't exactly a home improvement guru.

Then you start to chuckle, remembering one of your family's favorite Christmas movies. You send a quick text to your spouse, including this morning's hastily-taken photos of your home so full of sweet memories.

"It's a wonderful life, honey. I love you."

Hand on your heart, you do one last check-in of your inner peace.

JOURNAL PROMPTS

∞ *At one point in my journey I would sometimes use a mechanical hand counter clicker to "catch myself" each time I'd return back to mindful reality. It was a humble reminder at how rarely we come back to the present moment as we are learning. Don't be discouraged. Mindful moments only have to last a matter of seconds to pop us out of our crazy thoughts and back into physical reality. Each time you "wake up" into the present moment, what does it feel like?*

∞ *Jot down a few people whom you've honestly attempted to forgive. What do you think causes us to hold on to unforgiveness? Can you think of ways you can use photography to make peace with yourself and others?*

After getting these images home and working on them, a metaphor came up that led to a beautiful meditation. I thought of the walls I had built from unforgiveness. They represented "my story" and were beautiful and familiar in their own way. But, they held me back and cemented me as a victim. Never did I see the bridge overhead of forgiveness and letting go. We are commanded to forgive, and it is for our own spiritual progress that we do.

PHOTO TIP: MACRO TO SUPER-WIDE

The photos on this page make use of all three lenses on my iPhone—13 mm, 24 mm, and 77 mm, along with the macro mode feature. Embrace the creative potential of your smartphone and the scene you are standing in by making use of all lenses, macro to super-wide. Noticed how engaged you are while beautifully describing a place.

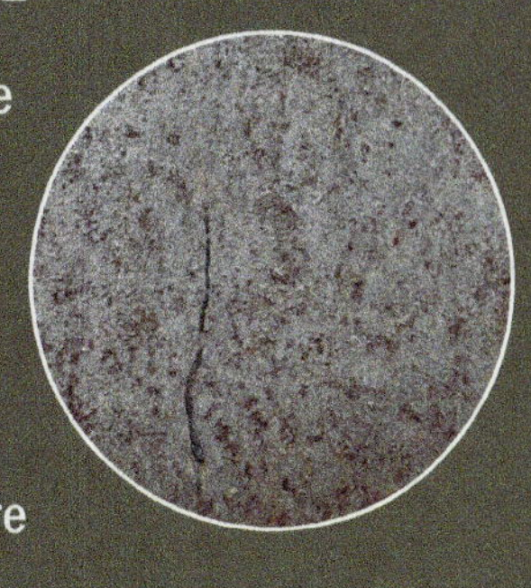

PRAISE

"Praise ye him, sun and moon:
praise him, all ye stars of light."

PSALM 148:3

What is the connection between praise and letting go? How can mindful photography inspire awe and help you rise above your hurts and expectations? How can a practice of praise transform your outlook on God, life, and your everyday problems?

LET'S EXPLORE

Praising your Higher Power is an act of humility as you set aside your own obsessions for a moment and simply praise the Spirit for this splendid moment right here, right now. The effect on the body's chemicals is instantaneous. All it takes is the act of turning from thought to the ego-transcendent state where new power and revelation can flow into your spirit. It also helps to be willing to dance around like a crazy maniac.

(left) I call it "forest lettuce." Deep in the woods you'll find it in early summer, grown tall like this. I distinctly remember coming across this scene, mind-blown, raising my hands in praise. I praise. You praise. The stars of light praise. And in their brief lifetime, stretched towards the sun, the forest lettuce praises the Almighty Creator of all things. Take a risk. Experience what it feels like to lift your hands high and praise.

This was shot with the super-wide (13mm) lens on an iPhone. I love being able to choose between 3 primes on a smartphone. See how the bottom of the frame is pointing straight down, yet we also see the tree-tops? For this effect, get in super-close, phone tilted downward.

What does praise look and feel like to you? Do you feel your most intense sense of awe while walking through a winter forest with snowflakes kissing your cheeks? Or perhaps you are a person who goes to a lively church and lifts your hands up in praise on Sunday mornings.

We're not talking about simple gratitude here. This practice combines gratitude with words and sounds of awe. For example, our winter forest person may raise their hands and yell "I love you!" over and over into the breathtaking snowy forest. Or, our Sunday morning worshiper may sing to God with tears of joy and hands raised, transcending self-consciousness.

I love to praise. Singing praise songs at the top of my lungs lifts me to a higher plane. It is one of the rare moments when I don't care what people think of me. I just want to be in awe of God through music.

Thousands of years ago, King David had a reputation for worshiping like nothing else mattered. One day he celebrated, shouting and playing trumpets in gratitude and praise to God in no-telling what state of dress. His wife got on his case for being vulgar, but David didn't apologize. "I will celebrate before the Lord. I will become even more undignified than this" (2 Samuel 6:21-22). Go David go! (By the way, I don't recommend smack-talk like this at home when your spouse reminds you to put your clothes back on.)

I encourage you to find and feel your own sense of praise. Tune in to healthy ways you become ecstatic, and turn them into fun and natural habits. Then, look for opportunities to capture photos of those moments while you are in a state of praise. Imagine our winter forest person reviewing a photo she captured right after shouting praise that day. That rich, joyful energy comes back to life every time she sees that captured memory.

1. FOCUS on body and surroundings

• HAND ON HEART • 3 BELLY BREATHS • NOTE YOUR LEVEL OF PEACE • OPEN YOUR EYES

With your eyes closed or gazing softly, gently place your hand on your heart and take three deep belly breaths. Simply feel your various body sensations. Note your level of inner peace. Open your eyes wide and take in what is surrounding you. Just "be" for a few seconds without commentary or categorizations.

2. CAPTURE the present moment

• ACT OPPOSITE TO EMOTION • TURN SMARTPHONE INTO CAMERA • PHOTOGRAPH MINDFULLY • NOTE YOUR LEVEL OF PEACE

Note your resistance to this practice and choose action anyway. Demonstrate your aim to experience inner peace by turning your smartphone into a camera, with airplane mode on. Now, wipe off your lenses and get your body to the best place to capture a few praiseworthy, mindful shots. What makes your heart leap with joy? Photograph that. Remain present while editing, capturing the look of the moment. Delete all but a few sacred photos. Pronounce your collection "complete" and do another hand-on-heart check-in of your inner peace.

3. SHINE your light on someone

• LOVE SOMEONE • STAY OFF SOCIAL MEDIA • NOTE YOUR LEVEL OF PEACE

Given that praise is towards the ultimate source of love and life, you are offering these images up to the Heavens. Ready to transcend the enticing familiarity of self-pity and fear? Dance and shout praise!

You'll deepen your connection with your personal God, sharing this intimate moment in the here and now. Refrain from sharing your praise representations on social media. Instead, keep them as a private offering to acknowledge God's love for you. Notice how you get lost in the moment when you connect with the spirit of praise. Hand on your heart, do one last check-in of your inner peace.

JOURNAL PROMPTS

∞ *Faced with an all-consuming problem, have you ever had someone tell you, "Just let it go!?" Did that feel like an impossible suggestion? Why?*

∞ *What does "praise" look like to you? How might you photograph that?*

∞ *How might a visually-amplified practice of praise transform your outlook on God, life, and your everyday problems?*

Praise God for the ice-covered lakes on Colorado's Grande Mesa, the Crystal River valley view from McLure Pass, the vivid red rocks of Glenwood Springs, and the explosive fall views of Keblar Pass en route to Crested Butte. It isn't a coincidence that experiences like this make our souls sing with praise. We were built to feel the beauty of creation. When encountering scenes of splendor, take time to sit and soak it in with all your senses, before even raising your camera.

PHOTO TIP: LEAVE THE PHONE IN THE CAR

There is a hilarious scene in National Lampoon's *Vacation* where Clark Griswold only allows his family a few panicked seconds to soak in the view of the Grand Canyon. Today that same scene would likely play out at a scenic view with the addition of a few puckering selfies. Sometimes it's a pleasant experience to skip the photo, breathe, and simply *be* with what's in front of you.

g. Erste Ansiedelung (Blockhaus) in Kentuc

LOVE

Our final section is the most mysterious of all. The feeling of love in all its forms is difficult to describe, much less define. But, aimed at magnifying love in our lives, we are up for the challenge.

After you live a few years, you observe that material things eventually deteriorate and dissolve away. But what lingers on? That is what these mindful photography practices will help you discover. You will learn to place attention on the only thing in the universe that transcends time and space: love.

Just about everything deteriorates: money, memory, our bodies, romantic love—nothing seems immune.

When you live in the western mountains as I do, you notice lots of falling-down log cabins in the landscape. It always sends a chill down my spine to see them. In very recent history—not much more than a century ago—a family built one of those cabins and lived out their lives, with all its stories of joys and sorrows. But now, all physical evidence of their existence is turning to dust.

If this relentless deterioration happens to material things, what remains?

THE ANSWER IS LOVE

When you are mindful of physical impermanence, you naturally begin to direct your energy towards the everlasting, which is love. Fortunately, the effects of a person's love keep shining after they pass from this physical plane, even though all material evidence of the person vanishes.

Let's get back to our family from the late 1800s, who built a cabin and settled on some land in the Utah mountains. The once beautiful cabin has deteriorated over the years. Grandmother and Grandfather lived out the rest of their days there, and the kids moved on, never returning to the cabin. A couple of decades later, the roof of the abandoned cabin collapsed. Today, the place isn't even fit for varmints.

Imagine being at that spot, surrounded by rolling hills of wheat, ripe for the harvest. You're on a road trip out west. Your curiosity drew you here, and now, standing next to this pile of notched logs, you are trying to wrap your head around this story that seemingly vanished without a trace.

Then, you lift your head and focus on the tiny town way off in the distance that you passed through on your way here. Your stomach tingles as you remember the plaque you read on the main street of the settlement, right in front of the little white church. The historical sign commemorated the town's namesakes, who settled and spread throughout the region, raising families and farming the fertile land.

Might you be standing at the genesis of this settlement? Was this the original spark of love that propagated through the region?

What a great time for a mindful shot. Hand on heart, you take a few belly breaths and check in with your level of presence. Before you even clean your lenses, the shot occurs to you. This time you'll shoot with the telephoto lens in order to compress the scene. You stand way back and capture the cabin rubble, softly focused on one side of the frame, and in the distance, the settlement is the focal point. You do a quick edit and place your mindful photo in a folder called Love Endures.

You do another little heart-check, breathing in the love that exists here, transcending time and space. An elderly friend and confidant back home comes to your mind—someone who could probably use a gift of love right now. The cell signal is weak, but you manage to send off a text with your mindful photo and a short note: Love endures forever.

Let's get mindful about love and all its dimensions. Precisely, what does love feel like in the body? How can you photograph that? What causes love-feelings to happen? How can you use mindful photography to reproduce love sensations, especially while you are in emotional trouble? Finally, we'll ask the most important question of all: "What is eternal love, and how do I receive it?"

LASTING LOVE

Cornell Psychologist Robert J. Sternberg developed the Triangular Theory of Love, proposing that love is composed of three distinct but interrelated components: intimacy, passion, and decision/commitment.

"The emotional intimacy and the cognitive decision/commitment components are typically rather constant in close relationships; once they are established in a relationship they are apt to endure. However, passion is considered to be less stable and much less predictable.

Within this theory, individuals love each other to the extent that they experience and evidence these three components, and different combinations of the components will yield markedly different kinds of love."[20]

Who would have thunk it? Can you relate to intimacy and commitment outlasting passion? Do you most identify with intimacy, passion, or commitment?

FEEL LOVE

*"You know you're in love
when you can't fall asleep
because reality is finally
better than your dreams."*

Dr. Seuss

Feel love and you will find mindfulness. Anyone who has felt the spark of love knows what it's like to come alive in the body. Love is the source of all life. Feeling and magnifying love in your body-core is tapping into the greatest power of the universe.

The love "frequency" is all around you. Cuddle with your pet for a moment and tell them how much they mean to you. That's the wavelength of love. Give your child a big smooch on the cheek and tell them they mean the world to you. How does that feel in your body? You just tuned to the FM radio station L-O-V-E.

Whether you are aware of the cause and effect, your plethora of emotions trigger corresponding body sensations. Bringing mindful awareness to the interplay of emotions and body sensations is a powerful tool in the process of recovery, because it places you as the observer of the thought-storms, rather than in the vortex of them.

Any human knows the unmistakable feeling of love. The ability to mindfully identify how love feels is key to predictably reproducing it.

Scientists have devised a series of maps revealing where in the body people feel love. In a study at Aalto University in Finland, researchers asked participants how they experience 27 types of love, including romantic love, sexual love, parental love, as well as love for friends, strangers, nature, God, and themselves.[21] They were then asked to pinpoint where they felt the love in their bodies, along with how intensely the feelings were physically and mentally.

Participants felt all types of love strongly in the head, but differed elsewhere. They found that the more strongly a type of love sensation is felt in the body, the more powerfully it is felt in the mind (and the more pleasant it is).

For example, they found that a mother's love for her child is centered in the heart, while people's love of nature tends to be focused in the head. For many, God was the most intensely experienced love of all.

You can use mindful photography to get specific with your own body map of love. Now it's time to get silly, have some laughs, and in the process, learn more about the most powerful force in the universe, capable of lifting us above all fear and suffering.

SCENARIO:

You're feeling low on love. Your spouse has been cold as a cucumber, calls to the kids are going to voicemail, and even your ugly mutt seems to be avoiding you.

1. FOCUS on body and surroundings

• HAND ON HEART • 3 BELLY BREATHS • NOTE YOUR LEVEL OF PEACE • OPEN YOUR EYES

During a time of meditation, with your eyes closed or gazing softly, gently place your hand on your heart and take three deep belly breaths. Simply feel your overall body sensations. Note your level of inner peace. Now allow your mind to land on a subject of love (perhaps your spouse, dog, child, or even nature), and point to the associated body sensations you are experiencing. Have fun with this; your body will react very quickly.

Of course, you can do this practice in the wild too. Imagine you are at a stoplight, thinking about a hot night out on the town last night with your sweetie. Point to where you are experiencing love in your body. Ahem! The light just turned green.

Or, imagine you just flopped on your bed and started snuggling with your dog. Catch yourself in the moment and get mindful. What are you feeling in your body? Where are the tingles? Is your heart beating? As you point to that spot, breathe into it, like you are fanning the flame of love sensations.

Really go for it. Think about all the things you love; they don't have to be profound. Right now, for instance, I am looking over at an old Leica M6 film camera of mine up on the shelf. It's a pain to shoot rangefinders. Loading and unloading it is tricky. Film and processing are expensive. Despite all of this—and I know it's silly— but I love that camera.

At this moment, I gently close my eyes and picture my Leica on the shelf, holding that energy in my consciousness. Here come the sensations. I point to a tingle in my lower belly. I rehearse memories of doing street photography with that camera. I think of the German craftsmanship of the nostalgic device. There's a tingling in the front of my face. I point to that. My mouth is curving upward. Another memory comes up and I feel pressure from my eyes wanting to tear up. I point there. I'm here now as one integrated being, body, mind, and spirit. Pretty enlightened, eh?

Now is when things get silly.

2. CAPTURE the present moment

• ACT OPPOSITE TO EMOTION • TURN SMARTPHONE INTO CAMERA • PHOTOGRAPH MINDFULLY • NOTE YOUR LEVEL OF PEACE

Demonstrate your aim to experience inner peace by turning your smartphone into a camera, with airplane mode on. Now, wipe off your lenses and get your body to the best place to capture a few mindful shots.

Note your resistance to having childlike fun with this practice. Choose action anyway. Get to a place where you can be weird, because you are getting ready to photograph some of your body parts. Don't worry, this is all G-rated content. In practicing this, especially with laughter and levity, you'll burn into your memory the connection between love thoughts and corresponding body sensations.

Back to my "love my Leica" moment, I start taking my silly body parts photos of the places I pointed to. I switch my camera to selfie mode. I just felt that tingling feeling in my lower belly; time for a belly button shot! I can feel the grin on my face. Time for a closeup of my curved lips. The pressure behind my eyes is back in a joyful way. I shoot horizontally, just showing my closed eyes.

I continue to be present while editing, deleting all but a few sacred photos that put a smile on my face. Finally, I file them away in a scandalous photo folder named "body parts."

It's time for one last hand-on-heart check-in. I catch myself aware of how the tingles of humor are filling my heart right now.

3. SHINE your light on someone

• LOVE SOMEONE • STAY OFF SOCIAL MEDIA • NOTE YOUR LEVEL OF PEACE

The "someone" in this practice is you. Jesus talked about the need to become like children in order to enter the kingdom of heaven (consciousness). You just tried something zany, aiming at transcending the usual in a humorously vulnerable way. In the process, you supercharged the conscious connection of where love shows up in your body. Notice how you get lost in the moment when you connect with your heart, lost in love. Keep noticing love sensations. Marvel at how we are all made to feel and be love. Hand on your heart, do one last check-in of your inner peace.

JOURNAL PROMPTS

∞ *Where do the body sensations associated with love show up in your body?*

∞ *How does the silly act of photographing body parts connect feelings of love to different sensations?*

∞ *"We are all made to feel and be love." Do you believe that? Why or why not? How can a mindful photography practice help amplify love in this moment?*

It's simple. Searching for photos that represent the feeling of love produces more love sensations inside. When you feel the tingles of love, slow down and breathe directly into those locations. Feel love expand and magnify inside your body. It's almost as if we can train our bodies to reproduce sensations of love. My parents in the center photo were together for 62 years of happy marriage. Frankie and me? We are going on 5 years of bliss.

LOOKIN' FOR LOVE

"I was lookin' for love in all the wrong places
Lookin' for love in too many faces
Searchin' their eyes, lookin' for traces
Of what I'm dreamin' of
Hoping to find a friend and a lover
I'll bless the day I discover another heart
Lookin' for love"

"Lookin' For Love" song by Johnny Lee

Consider someone like Larry King, married 5 or more times. What keeps people like Larry repeating the same patterns, looking for love in all the wrong places? This pattern isn't just a modern phenomenon. In the book of John in the New Testament, we hear the story of Jesus seeking out the woman at the well. "Why would a Jew talk to a lowly, disgraced Samaritan woman?" she asked Jesus. Jesus revealed that he knew everything about her, including all her previous husbands. He offered her an eternal solution: living water.

I believe that the living water Jesus offered was the Love of God, available to all of us right here at this moment. None of our fulfilled earthly desires can come close to the feeling of being filled with divine love.

If real love doesn't look like worldly stuff, then what does it look like? Can you even see it? Can you touch it? Does it have mass? Probably not. But you can capture the effects of love. Bringing up the feeling of this mysterious force is a skill you can master through mindful acts of love, using your camera.

In the previous practice, you got funky and took shots of areas of your body where you can feel love. Connecting love to specific body sensations is an important prerequisite to the "Lookin' for Love" practice, because being tuned into those love sensations will show you what to photograph.

Has your spouse ever responded to a vulnerable moment of yours with a soft, encouraging touch? Photograph their hand in a beautiful way. Does it soothe your soul to snuggle with your pooch? Photograph their fur touching your skin. What are other ways you can capture an abstract concept like love?

As I write this, I am sipping coffee from a Snoopy coffee mug that my now-deceased mother gave me last Christmas. I think I'll capture a shot and send a love note to her in heaven. The crazy thing is, just the thought of doing that conjures up love feelings inside me.

These practice ideas will help you learn to use your camera as a freeing tool for yourself, and simultaneously as a means to bless others and magnify the love inside you both.

John Lennon vocalized some of the truest words of all time: "The love you take is equal to the love you make." Let's use that as guidance in this mindful photography practice.

LOOKIN' FOR LOVE IN ALL THE *RIGHT* PLACES

In the pitiful "Lookin' For Love" song by Johnny Lee, we see the singer's desperate attempts to find love outside of himself to fill the void left by yet another lost romance. He dreams of one day finding a match with someone equally as heart-sick. Is it just me, or does 'ol Johnny seem to be stuck on repeat, chasing love solely for his own gratification?

I turn into a Johnny Lee all the time, looking for what I can get out of love, versus how I can serve others to foster love within them and consequentially, inside me. When I am mindfully aware, I'll quickly catch myself acting with the motive of "getting" love. In my better moments, I'll consciously switch into John Lennon mode, realizing that the love I take is equal to the love I make—and that comes in the form of service.

The idea of serving others through mindful photography is not an afterthought. In fact, it is the single most important part of these practices; that's why I've included the "Shine Your Light on Someone" step at the end of each practice. Service is love in action.

I know first-hand that the last thing I want to do when I'm in a lonely funk is to reach out and serve my fellows. "I have no love left to give—it's me that needs the love right now," I will insist. When those thoughts arrive, I know they are not the path to peaceful, inner relief. Depression is often called a "disease of isolation." When down, most people tend to cut themselves off from people and activities that give them the very loving connections that their souls yearn for.

If you truly want to step from the shore of malaise into the powerful current of God's love, consider some of these ideas.

DISCOVER YOUR (PHOTOGRAPHIC) SERVICE GIFTING

While serving in a church community years back, I did a group Bible study about spiritual gifts. At another faith community I got deep into the Enneagram, which has roots in the early church. These types of studies have always fascinated me, particularly because they focus on me (my favorite subject). Once I get past that, I discover something far deeper. Yes, working within my spiritual gifting is gratifying. But what makes it transformational is connecting my gifts to the needs in front of me. Like a plug in a socket, when I serve someone I am jacked into God's powerful current of energy and peace.

Have fun with an online personality test, and perhaps a spiritual gifting test. Alternatively, ask a trusted friend where you seem to shine. You were created with unique gifts and propensities, and you are designed to fit into a whole. Community doesn't always come naturally; it is the reward of investing in others. Use your love of photography to search out ways to serve that make you come alive. Being in the groove and creating works of art feels mighty mindful. And, it represents love in action.

SHOOT PUPPIES

No, for goodness' sakes, not that kind of shoot. *Photograph* puppies. Dogs and cats too. Your local animal shelter has a constant need for great pet portraits. An amazing photographer in a city I lived in volunteered to capture dog portraits at a shelter. The dogs he photographed were adopted much more quickly than the dogs with standard shots. His next-level shots got picked up by the press. Before you know it, this guy's whole career changed and he is known far and wide for his dog portraits.

CAPTURE PORTRAITS FOR A CAUSE

Numerous organizations need fresh people-shots for their social media. You can help. Portraiture is my favorite form of photography, probably because of its therapeutic effect on me. It forces me into deeply personal interaction with the subject, and those unpredictably creative moments in a portrait session are intensely mindful. Serving others through portraits doesn't have to be an ambitious act for a group. How about going out into nature with a friend who is launching a new website in need of some mindful portraits?

ROCK YOUR CAMERA; BLESS A BAND

Up-and-coming bands are so appreciative of live-performance photos from fans. While living in Austin, this act of love was so gratifying to me, particularly while I was feeling low and disconnected. I'd gear up with my full frame camera and a fast 35mm lens, and go out to one of my favorite honky-tonks, like the Continental

Club on South Congress. Getting uncomfortably close and capturing small-venue live music is a rush indeed. Sometimes I'd even hop up on the back of the stage and shoot towards the crowd. As fun as the rush of adrenaline was in the moment, the rush of love came later. The times when I emailed bands links to a carefully-curated and edited folder full of images made me feel fun and loving connections with others who appreciate art and artists. Even some of the most brilliant, hard-working bands can struggle to make a go of it. You can put a smile on their faces by giving them live-action photos to share with their fans while promoting their next gig. That's love, and rocking your camera is very, very mindful.

HELP A SELFIE

I love to visit an enormous hot springs pool in the mountain town where I live. Some days when I go there, I get to observe a little old lady named Dolly, acting out her ministry. I call it a ministry because by now she has probably blessed a thousand or more tourists from all walks of life and all corners of the planet. Her service is simple. The moment she sees a couple taking a selfie, or a family awkwardly trying to get everyone into a shot, she's on them like a spandex bathing suit. Next thing you know, Dolly has one of their smartphones in hand, directing them just so, snapping away. She knows all the great angles to best show off the people in the pool, while capturing the mountains in the background. I smile every time I see this act of love and ponder how many families around the world, because of Dolly, feel the love of that memory at our hot springs pool in the mountains. The next time you feel a tug on your heart to make a loving memory for someone, help a selfie. I promise you'll be fully mindful during the scene that unfolds, and you'll walk away feeling the rush of love that comes from taking a risk.

SHOW SOMEONE WHAT THEY MEAN TO YOU

Do you remember the last time you received a personal, handwritten letter in the mail? Can you remember the feelings of love that came from that gesture? Imagine that inside that envelope was also a selfie of the two of you at a special getaway. There is something special about our jagged handwriting. It takes such effort to print a photo and then write, seal, and mail a letter. But the effect is pure and eternal love. Find your own unique ways to create loving impacts. That friend who you took shots of in the forest? Send her a pack of custom note cards with her portrait to send to her new clients. She will think of your kind act each time she uses her special gift. Let's not forget about mom, dad, or any adult who remembers film cameras. Order some prints online and have them sent directly. You'll make their day, and those memories will amplify the love you share.

SCENARIO:

You're walking down the street, head hanging low, looking for the nearest pity party. Next thing you know, your head is swinging back and forth and you are humming Ray Charles and singing, "If it wasn't for bad luck I wouldn't have any luck at all." "Oh brother," you say with a frown as you walk past a family of tourists, fumbling around trying to take a group selfie. Something stops you dead in your tracks and you do an about face. The Spirit convicted you. It's "help-a-selfie" time!

1. FOCUS on body and surroundings

• HAND ON HEART • 3 BELLY BREATHS • NOTE YOUR LEVEL OF PEACE • OPEN YOUR EYES

In that split second when you turned around to help that sweet family, you were aware that your level of inner peace was waning and you wanted to intervene. You made a quick decision to bless others and share the loving light of God.

2. CAPTURE the present moment

• ACT OPPOSITE TO EMOTION • TURN SMARTPHONE INTO CAMERA • PHOTOGRAPH MINDFULLY • NOTE YOUR LEVEL OF PEACE

Even while in a funk, you spontaneously choose action anyway. You demonstrated your aim to experience inner peace through stepping out of your comfort zone and helping people in need.

Place your hand on your heart now and then, noting your level of inner peace. Feel all the flutters and tingles inside. Take a moment here and there to breathe into the good feelings.

3. SHINE your light on someone

• LOVE SOMEONE • STAY OFF SOCIAL MEDIA • NOTE YOUR LEVEL OF PEACE

All these ideas about eternal love are about you shining your light to bless others. Are you ready to transcend the enticing familiarity of self-pity and fear? Commit to a mindful photography practice and touch someone with your gifts. You'll create loving connections and redirect your attention to the eternal. Refrain from sharing your creations on social media. Instead, bless someone directly with your photos. Notice how you get lost in the moment when you connect with someone's heart. Hand on your heart, do one last check-in of your inner peace.

JOURNAL PROMPTS

∞ *Where do you tend to look for love in all the wrong places? Describe them non-judgmentally.*

∞ *How can you use mindful photography to observe love?*

∞ *Our example was of a person whose mood shifted immediately as a result of turning towards love, rather than avoiding love. It goes to show that our emotions come and go. How have you experienced freedom through giving love, even when you didn't feel like it?*

Sometimes I'll walk through nature scenes like this and feel totally cocooned by God's love. I am lovingly fine-tuned to appreciate the glory of creation. After all, creation and I are one.

Been lookin' for love in all the wrong places? Welcome to my world. Sometimes I'll get that needy, longing feeling inside, searching for a way to get me some l-o-v-e. Invariably, I strike out because I have my camera lens on backwards. Once I bring awareness to this familiar pattern, I'll say to my lower-self, "Remember? You've got to give it to get it. Sorry self, that's just how the Universe works."

There is always someone out there in need of God's touch. When I feel that inner nudge to reach out, that means God needs my hands at that moment to pull off someone's miracle. And, being someone's angel feels mighty good down deep inside. Don't believe me? Place your hand on your heart and take three belly breaths. Allow someone to come to your mind who could use a loving touch. Without hesitation, pick a beautiful photo and send them a text with a few words of encouragement.

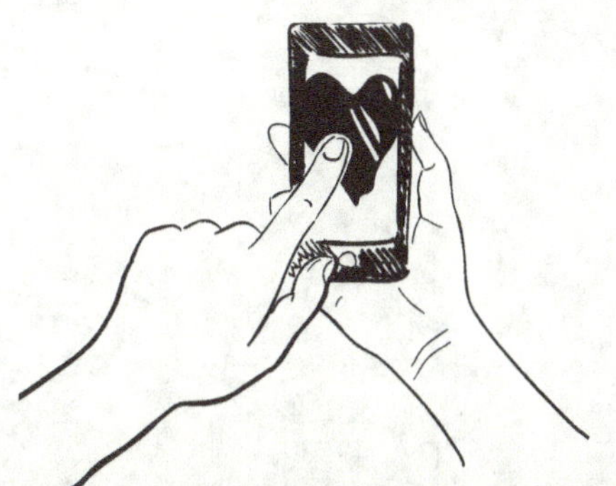

ETERNAL LOVE

"Love is eternal. There are inspired messages, but they are temporary; there are gifts of speaking in strange tongues, but they will cease; there is knowledge, but it will pass."

1 CORINTHIANS 13:8

In this final practice, you will utilize mindful photography to explore the eternality of love. Absolutely nothing compares to the healing effect of tapping into pure, eternal love.

If you are not of Christian belief, or if your Christian interpretations are different from mine, please look past my bias. The only way I can be completely honest with you is to tell you about my personal (and at times painful) experience with God. In my long walk of faith, I have never found anyone with my same views and practices, but we all seem to share some of the same basic beliefs.

People of faith, eastern-practitioners, twelve steppers, agnostics, and anyone else regardless of your personal beliefs—join me in this practice. Let's pursue the things we can all agree on—things like freedom of practice, our desire for peace, and the deep yearning of the human spirit to connect with a higher power.

A lot of mighty smart people purport that love is simply a powerful emotion coupled with an essential physiological drive. Others have a different take, pointing out that love behaves differently than emotions, which typically increase or decrease in response to our

(left) Who would have known that this young boy, poor in possessions but rich in love, would turn out to be our mother's caring husband of 62 years, and the loving father of my siblings and me. Dad led us in the way of love, and now that love is impacting generations.

environment. These people argue that love seems to manifest in a more constant and transcendent way. In contrast, popular culture defines love as lustful and conditional.

People of faith point to how important love is to God. Why would love be important to God? Because God is everlasting love, available to walk with us and talk with us at any moment. Whatever your personal belief, I hope you are able to use these "Eternal Love" mindful photography ideas to deepen your focus on a personal, everlasting love, and to participate in it, one day at a time.

SCENARIO:

This is a perfect practice for your morning quiet time. Whether you journal or just sit in silence, embrace the inspiration in front of you. Open yourself up to divine peace and inner healing. You'll tap into the most powerful force in the universe as you commit to pursuing eternal love for that one day.

1. FOCUS on body and surroundings

• **HAND ON HEART** • **3 BELLY BREATHS** • **NOTE YOUR LEVEL OF PEACE**
• **OPEN YOUR EYES**

During your sacred time, with your eyes closed or gazing softly, gently place your hand on your heart and take three deep belly breaths. Simply feel your various body sensations. Note your level of inner peace. Open your eyes wide and take in what is surrounding you. Just "be" for a few seconds without commentary or categorizations.

Ready to take a risk? Say a prayer. A big prayer. Out loud. Ask your God, your higher power, or the universe to lead you towards eternal love today. Ask that you be shown little miracles of love that you've previously overlooked. Ask that your whole life purpose be centered in the eternal. Ask God to relieve you from earthly identifications, so that through these mindful moments you can focus on what really counts. You can be confident that a life lived like this will produce the most abundant fruit imaginable.

2. CAPTURE the present moment

• ACT OPPOSITE TO EMOTION • TURN SMARTPHONE INTO CAMERA
• PHOTOGRAPH MINDFULLY • NOTE YOUR LEVEL OF PEACE

Note your resistance to this practice and choose action anyway. Demonstrate your aim to experience inner peace by turning your smartphone into a camera, with airplane mode on. Now, wipe off your lenses and get your body to the best place to capture a few mindful shots.

The "Eternal Love" practice instructions couldn't be any simpler: Go through this day capturing shots of things that will pass away eventually. Take a snap of that old junker of a car you walk by on your way to work. Or how about a shot of a white puffy cloud above your head? Throughout your day, also take shots of symbolic things representing what eternal love means to you—things that do not pass away, but rather transcend time and space. Ask for divine guidance. Seek and you will find. Feel the effect these mindful photography practices are having on your soul.

Remain present while editing, capturing the look of the moment. Delete all but a few sacred photos. Pronounce your collection "complete" and add them to your Eternal Love folder.

Slide your hand on your heart again, and note your level of inner peace.

3. SHINE your light on someone

• LOVE SOMEONE • STAY OFF SOCIAL MEDIA • NOTE YOUR LEVEL OF PEACE

Are you ready to transcend the enticing familiarity of self-pity and fear? Shine your light and bless others through your mindful photos. Are some of these photos highly personal? Offer them up to God for transformation. Abandon yourself to the present moment. Create loving connections and redirect your attention to the eternal. Refrain from sharing your creations on social media. Instead, bless someone directly with your photos. Notice how you get lost in the moment when you connect with someone's heart. Hand on your heart, do one last check-in of your inner peace.

JOURNAL PROMPTS

∞ *The idiom "you can't take it with you" tends to be directed towards people who hoard their money or possessions. When you take your last breath, what will you carry with you into the next life?*

∞ *What does "storing up treasures in Heaven" mean to you? Imagine you enter Heaven and God shows you your heavenly storage unit. What might be in there?*

∞ *With your unique gifts and ways of approaching the world, how can you practice producing eternal love through mindful photography?*

We are the offspring of pure, eternal love. But as a sad irony, that love is buried beneath a deep mound of twisted ego and pain from life's collective troubles. Fortunately, there are reliable shortcuts that tap us back into the source of eternal love. Prayer and service are two of the most powerful means of practicing loving presence.

PHOTO TIP: NEVER GIVE UP

Winston Churchill said this in a 1941 speech of defiance against tyranny: *"Never give in, never give in, never, never, never, never—in nothing, great or small, large or petty—never give in except to convictions of honour and good sense. Never yield to force: never yield to the apparently overwhelming might of the enemy."*

I pray that each of you practice presence vigilantly and rise up against the enemy's inner voice of discouragement. Always return to the light, claiming out loud that you will never, never, never give up.

REFERENCES

[1] "One in 100 Deaths Is by Suicide." World Health Organization, June 17, 2021. https://www.who.int/news/item/17-06-2021-one-in-100-deaths-is-by-suicide.

[2] Moutier, Christine. "Suicidal Behavior - Mental Health Disorders." Merck Manuals Consumer Version, August 2023. https://www.merckmanuals.com/home/mental-health-disorders/suicidal-behavior-and-self-injury/suicidal-behavior.

[3] "Suicide Statistics." American Foundation for Suicide Prevention, March 7, 2024. https://afsp.org/suicide-statistics/.

[4] "Facts about Suicide." Centers for Disease Control and Prevention, May 8, 2023. https://www.cdc.gov/suicide/facts/index.html.

[5] "2023 National Veteran Suicide Prevention Annual Report." US Department of Veterans Affairs, November 2023. https://www.mentalhealth.va.gov/docs/data-sheets/2023/2023-National-Veteran-Suicide-Prevention-Annual-Report-FINAL-508.pdf.

[6] Fahmy, Dalia. "Key Findings about Americans' Belief in God." Pew Research Center, April 25, 2018. https://www.pewresearch.org/short-reads/2018/04/25/key-findings-about-americans-belief-in-god/.

[7] Csikszentmihalyi, Mihaly. *Flow: The Psychology of Optimal Experience.* New York: Harper and Row, 2009.

[8] Stern, Daniel N. *The Present Moment in Psychotherapy and Everyday Life.* New York: W.W. Norton, 2004.

[9] Johnson, Douglas C, Nathaniel J Thom, Elizabeth A Stanley, Lori Haase, Alan N Simmons, Pei-An B Shih, Wesley K Thompson, Eric G Potterat, Thomas R Minor, and Martin P Paulus. "Modifying Resilience Mechanisms in At-Risk Individuals: A Controlled Study of Mindfulness Training in Marines Preparing for Deployment." The American journal of psychiatry, August 2014. https://www.ncbi.nlm.nih.gov/pmc/articles/PMC4458258/.

[10] Hölzel, Britta K., James Carmody, Mark Vangel, Christina Congleton, Sita M. Yerramsetti, Tim Gard, and Sara W. Lazar. "Mindfulness Practice Leads to Increases in Regional Brain Gray Matter Density." Psychiatry research, November 10, 2010. https://pubmed.ncbi.nlm.nih.gov/21071182/.

[11] Van Der Kolk, Bessel. *The Body Keeps the Score: Brain, Mind, and Body in the Healing of Trauma.* London: Penguin Books, 2015.

[12]Umejima, Keita, Takuya Ibaraki, Takahiro Yamazaki, and Kuniyoshi L. Sakai. "Paper Notebooks vs. Mobile Devices: Brain Activation Differences during Memory Retrieval." Frontiers, February 15, 2021. https://www.frontiersin.org/articles/10.3389/fnbeh.2021.634158/full.

[13]Duncan, Francesca E., Emily L. Que, Nan Zhang, Eve C. Feinberg, Thomas V. O'Halloran, and Teresa K. Woodruff. "The Zinc Spark Is an Inorganic Signature of Human Egg Activation." Nature News, April 26, 2016. https://www.nature.com/articles/srep24737.

[14]Kobayashi, Masaki, Daisuke Kikuchi, and Hitoshi Okamura. "Imaging of Ultraweak Spontaneous Photon Emission from Human Body Displaying Diurnal Rhythm." Plos One, July 16, 2009. https://journals.plos.org/plosone/article?id=10.1371%2Fjournal.pone.0006256.

[15]Walsh, Lisa C., Annie Regan, Jean M. Twenge, and Sonja Lyubomirsky. "What Is the Optimal Way to Give Thanks? Comparing the Effects of Gratitude Expressed Privately, One-to-One via Text, or Publicly on Social Media" Affective Science. SpringerLink, October 11, 2022. https://link.springer.com/article/10.1007/s42761-022-00150-5.

[16]Sexton, J Bryan, and Kathryn C Adair. "Forty-Five Good Things: A Prospective Pilot Study of the Three Good Things Well-Being Intervention in the USA for Healthcare Worker Emotional Exhaustion, Depression, Work–Life Balance and Happiness." BMJ Open, March 1, 2019. https://bmjopen.bmj.com/content/9/3/e022695.

[17]Chowdhury, Madhuleena Roy. "The Neuroscience of Gratitude and Effects on the Brain." PositivePsychology.com, April 9, 2019. https://positivepsychology.com/neuroscience-of-gratitude/.

[18]Tseng, Julie, and Jordan Poppenk. "Brain Meta-State Transitions Demarcate Thoughts across Task Contexts Exposing the Mental Noise of Trait Neuroticism." Nature News, July 13, 2020. https://www.nature.com/articles/s41467-020-17255-9.

[19]Ryback, Ralph. "The Powerful Psychology behind Cleanliness." Psychology Today, July 6, 2016. https://www.psychologytoday.com/us/blog/the-truisms-wellness/201607/the-powerful-psychology-behind-cleanliness.

[20]Anderson, Julius W. "Sternberg's Triangular Theory of Love." Wiley Online Library, March 17, 2016. https://onlinelibrary.wiley.com/doi/abs/10.1002/9781119085621.wbefs058.

[21]Rinne, Pärttyli, Mikke Tavast, Enrico Glerean, and Mikko Samms. "Where Do We Feel Love?" Aalto University, September 19, 2023. https://www.aalto.fi/en/news/where-do-we-feel-love.